# Sync or Swim

## Balancing Individuality and Togetherness in Relationships

Saloomeh Nakhsaz, LMFT

*For my late father,*

*In loving memory of a man who shaped my soul and guided my steps, whose love for me was a beacon in times of darkness. Dad, you made me feel heard and cherished, always there to shield me from life's storms with your wisdom and love.*

*Your humility and nonjudgmental spirit taught me the essence of true kindness. You sowed the seeds of compassion and service in my heart, touching lives and guiding souls without ever expecting anything in return.*

*In you, I found not just a father but a hero—a role model of boundless virtue, forever occupying a sacred space within my heart. You were the compass for every crucial decision in my life, and even now, in your physical absence, your influence persists.*

*Each day, I find myself pondering, "What would Dad do?" And in doing so, I honor your legacy. I am endlessly proud to be your daughter and eternally grateful for the joyous moments we shared, for the lessons learned at your feet, and for the countless times your voice and your face have been my sanctuary.*

*Words fail to capture the depth of my love and the chasm of my loss, but know this: You are missed beyond measure and loved beyond words. May you rest in eternal peace, Dad. My heart is forever indebted to you, and I carry your spirit with me always.*

*With boundless love and eternal gratitude,*

*-Saloomeh.*

# Acknowledgments

This book is the product of invaluable contributions from a wide range of individuals to whom I owe profound gratitude.

First and foremost, my esteemed clients deserve special recognition. Your courage and willingness to delve into the complexities of human relationships have significantly enriched this work. I consider it a privilege to have served as your therapist and confidant.

I extend my heartfelt gratitude to Edward Subega, my clinical mentor, during my volunteer tenure at the suicide and crisis center. Your authentic compassion and deep understanding of human psychology have provided invaluable dimensions to my approach to therapeutic engagement.

The intellectual contributions of experts such as Dr. Jordan Peterson, Dr. Gabor Mate, Sue Johnson, John and Julie Gottman, and Eckhart Tolle have been instrumental in shaping my perspective. Your groundbreaking works have served as essential guides for my professional development.

A special note of thanks goes to my son, Sam. Your relentless curiosity has been a catalyst in my ongoing intellectual journey, further enriched by your introductions to the works of Dr. Jordan Peterson and Eckhart Tolle.

I also acknowledge the philosophical contributions of the late Alan Watts, whose thoughts on human psychology and relationships continue to inform my work.

My mother, Zara, has been a constant source of inspiration and encouragement. Her unwavering belief in my capabilities propelled me toward the path of therapy even before I fully embraced it.

To Homayoon, my life partner, your limitless love and steadfast belief in my vision have made obstacles appear surmountable, transforming aspirations into achievements.

Lastly, to my children, Sam and Eli, you serve as the ever-present reminders of the beauty and complexity of human life. Your very existence enriches my professional and personal journey in immeasurable ways.

As I bring this acknowledgment to a close, I wish to express my heartfelt gratitude to each individual mentioned, as well as to the many others whose quiet yet significant contributions have enriched this work. In your own distinct ways, you have collectively crafted this complex and beautiful creation. It is my hope that this book will serve as an appropriate homage to the lasting impact you have all made.

With deepest respect and unending thanks,

Saloomeh

# Table of Contents

# Introduction

Welcome to a transformative journey—a journey that promises not just to alter the way you view relationships but also to equip you with the tools needed to build a lasting and fulfilling emotional bond with your partner. If you're reading this book, it's likely that you're interested in understanding the complexities of emotional interaction, the underpinnings of love, and the nuances that make a relationship both challenging and rewarding.

Relationships are not one-dimensional; they are intricate ecosystems that involve the interplay of multiple facets, such as emotional intelligence, communication skills, and personal boundaries. They are both the mirror reflecting our inner worlds and the window through which we explore the universe of another human being. Therefore, it is essential to approach them with the care, understanding, and strategy that they warrant.

In **Part I: The Cornerstones of Balanced Relationships**, we will delve into the dual nature of love. We will explore how autonomy and intimacy co-exist, how the journey to knowing your partner starts with understanding yourself, and the importance of crafting and sustaining personal boundaries.

Moving on to **Part II: Navigating the Rocky Terrain: Challenges and Roadblocks**, we will face the darker aspects head-on. We will dissect the quicksand of over-attachment to the isolation chambers of excessive individuality and provide you with a comprehensive framework for building emotional resilience—your relationship's ultimate defense system.

In **Part III: The Art of Relational Communication**, the focus shifts to the power of words and beyond. Learn to express your needs and desires while also developing the skills to listen actively and empathetically to your partner's perspective.

**Part IV: The Sustaining Forces: Rituals, Experiences, and Shared Values** serves as a treasure trove of ideas. Here, you will discover case studies and practical suggestions for activities that can enhance your connection while respecting each partner's individuality.

Finally, in **Part V: Conclusion**, we will summarize the key takeaways and outline the next steps on your ongoing journey toward relationship nirvana.

As you proceed through the chapters, remember that this book is not meant to be a quick fix but a guide for ongoing development. It provides not just theoretical knowledge but actionable steps designed to transform your relational dynamics. You're not just going to learn *what* makes relationships tick; you'll discover *how* to apply that knowledge in a practical way.

Embark on this enriching journey with an open heart and a committed mindset.

May your reading be enlightening and your relationship-building even more so.

# PART I

# The Cornerstones of Balanced Relationships

# 1

# The Enigmatic Interplay of Love: Autonomy and Intimacy Unveiled

In the intricate maze of human emotions and relationships, two foundational pillars stand firm yet paradoxical—autonomy and intimacy. Each serves as a beacon that illuminates a different path through the labyrinth of love, yet both are quintessential for achieving the truest forms of connection and self-realization. This chapter aims to function as a compass, offering nuanced insights into navigating this complex terrain where individuality and emotional unity coalesce in a seamless fabric.

## An In-depth Exploration of Human Psychological Needs

At the core of human well-being are three elemental needs outlined in self-determination theory: autonomy, competence, and relatedness. These underpinnings serve as scaffolds upon which the complex architecture of our psychological health is constructed. Autonomy acts as the internal GPS, empowering us to make choices that resonate with our deepest convictions and guiding us toward fulfilling our unique destinies. Competence awakens our innate quest to master our universe, allowing us to surmount challenges, solve problems, and relish the rewarding sensation of accomplishment. Finally, relatedness answers our primal call for emotional intimacy and belonging, drawing us into the communal web of interdependent relationships where reciprocity and emotional nourishment flourish.

## The Symbiotic Relationship of Autonomy and Intimacy in Love

It's in the sphere of romantic relationships that autonomy and relatedness intersect most dramatically. The union is not just physical or even emotional; it's a complex layering of individual aspirations, shared goals, personal boundaries, and collective experiences. Autonomy grants us the liberty to remain uniquely ourselves within the relationship, to pursue personal goals and passions, and to develop in ways that might be entirely separate from our partner. Intimacy, on the other hand, offers the sweet nectar of emotional communion, the shared language of hearts and minds, and the inimitable experience of being known and understood at our most vulnerable core.

## Autonomy as the Soil for Personal Evolution

Maintaining autonomy within relationships is not a mere accessory; it is the fertile soil from which the flower of individuality blooms. It cultivates the space for intellectual curiosity, emotional independence, and personal exploration. This private sphere allows us to venture out and then return, enriching the collective relationship experience with the fruits of our individual journeys.

## Intimacy: The Divine Conduit of Emotional Alchemy

Conversely, intimacy functions as the alchemical crucible where two souls can merge without losing their individual essence. It fosters an environment of emotional safety, encouraging the authentic expression of feelings, thoughts, and vulnerabilities. Intimacy nurtures and fortifies the relationship, transmuting it from a casual association into an emotionally rich, deeply satisfying, and spiritually enlightening connection.

## The Art of Equilibrium: The Dynamic Balance Between Two Worlds

In any relationship, keeping the scales balanced between autonomy and intimacy is an ongoing process—a dance choreographed to the rhythm of life's ever-changing scenarios. This equilibrium varies from person to person and from relationship to relationship, but its universal principle remains:

imbalance in either direction can lead to relationship dissatisfaction or personal emotional discord. Mastering this nuanced equilibrium is the key to nourishing relationships that both respect individual growth and celebrate collective emotional and spiritual abundance.

## A Prelude to the Journey Ahead

As you delve into the succeeding chapters of this book, you'll be equipped with actionable tactics, fortified by empirical psychological research, and provided with experiential exercises designed to help you deftly navigate the fascinating dichotomies of autonomy and intimacy. With this comprehensive understanding, you become more than just a traveler on the road of love; you become an astute navigator capable of steering through both placid and turbulent emotional waters.

So, as you turn the page, take with you a sense of adventure and a willingness to delve deep. This expedition into the caverns of emotional and psychological complexity is an enriching enterprise, promising a treasury of insights, revelations, and life-altering wisdom that has the power to redefine your understanding of love, deepen your relationships, and elevate your personal well-being.

# Real-Life Stories

*Disclaimer: All names and identifying details have been changed to protect confidentiality. The therapist referred to is the book's author.*

## Story 1: Emily and Ben - The Quest for Balance

Emily and Ben, both professionals in their early 30s, came to therapy with a sense of emotional disconnection despite a robust social life and shared interests. Emily, an independent entrepreneur, craved more autonomy, feeling that the relationship had started to suffocate her space for personal growth. Ben, on the other hand, felt a strong need for emotional intimacy that he believed was lacking.

Upon diving deeper into self-determination theory, they both recognized that their relationship was off-kilter in satisfying their fundamental psychological needs. They worked through exercises that helped them define boundaries and articulate their needs for both autonomy and intimacy.

After a few months of conscious effort, they discovered a newfound equilibrium. Emily felt she could breathe, explore, and still belong; Ben felt emotionally connected, appreciated, and still free.

## Story 2: Sophia - Reclaiming Autonomy

Sophia, a middle-aged woman, found herself struggling after her long-term relationship ended. She had invested so much into the intimacy of her relationship that she lost sight of her autonomous self. She had to relearn her individuality, set new personal goals, and separate her identity from being one-half of a couple.

Through a series of self-reflective exercises and deep psychological probing, Sophia slowly embraced her autonomy. She rekindled her love for painting, a passion she had long shelved. As she explored this forgotten part of herself, she also found that she could engage in new relationships with a greater sense of self, thus enriching her capacity for intimacy without sacrificing her autonomy.

## Story 3: Alex and Taylor - Rediscovering Intimacy

Alex and Taylor, a married couple in their late 40s, had a seemingly perfect relationship with successful careers and two wonderful kids. However, they had become more like roommates than romantic partners. Both were autonomous to the point that intimacy was severely lacking. They missed the emotional closeness they once had but didn't know how to reclaim it.

With a focus on the need for intimacy to complement autonomy, they started re-engaging in shared activities that once brought them joy. They instigated a "no phones" policy during dinner and started attending a weekly dance class together. In these shared spaces, they rediscovered their emotional connection. They learned to communicate openly about their feelings, fears, and desires, thus revitalizing the lost intimacy.

## Story 4: Jordan - The Solo Journey to Balanced Selfhood

Jordan, in their late 20s, had always struggled with setting boundaries, often yielding to the needs and expectations of others, be it family or romantic partners. The quest for intimacy seemed to always overpower their own needs for personal space and autonomy.

Through cognitive behavioral therapy exercises focusing on self-determination theory, Jordan identified this pattern and committed to change. They began to actively practice saying 'no,' valuing their own time and pursuing individual hobbies. By doing so, Jordan realized that their relationships actually improved; they could offer emotional closeness without feeling drained or losing their sense of self.

*These stories demonstrate the variety of ways the principles of autonomy and intimacy manifest in real-life scenarios. By understanding and applying the principles outlined in this chapter, each individual or couple took significant steps toward more fulfilling, balanced, and emotionally rich relationships.*

## Recommended Exercises

Exercise 1: Mapping Your Autonomy and Intimacy Needs

- **Objective**: To identify your personal needs for autonomy and intimacy.
- **Instructions**:
- List five activities or aspects of life where you desire more autonomy.
- List five activities or aspects of life where you seek deeper intimacy with your partner.
- **Discussion**: Share your lists with your partner and discuss ways you can support each other in these areas.

Exercise 2: Boundaries Audit

- **Objective**: To examine and possibly redefine boundaries within the relationship.
- **Instructions**:
- Each partner writes down what they consider to be their non-negotiable boundaries.
- Share and discuss these with your partner.

- **Discussion**: Are there areas where boundaries can be adjusted to create more autonomy or intimacy? Make an action plan.

Exercise 3: Weekly Check-In Ritual

- **Objective**: To build a consistent space for open dialogue about needs and feelings.
- **Instructions**:
- Set aside 20-30 minutes each week for an open conversation.
- Discuss what felt balanced this week and what did not in terms of autonomy and intimacy.
- **Discussion**: Develop strategies for the upcoming week to work on imbalances.

Exercise 4: 'Me Time' and 'We Time' Planning

- **Objective**: To consciously allocate time for individual and shared activities.
- **Instructions**:
- Use a calendar to mark out specific times for 'Me Time' for each partner and 'We Time' for shared activities.
- **Discussion**: At the end of the week, review how well the plan worked and adjust as necessary.

Exercise 5: Emotional Availability Scale

- **Objective**: To gauge and understand the levels of emotional availability between partners.

- **Instructions**:
- On a scale of 1-10, rate how emotionally available you feel to your partner and how emotionally available your partner is to you.
- Share your ratings.
- **Discussion**: Discuss the reasons for your ratings and what can be done to increase emotional availability if needed.

Exercise 6: The Freedom-Connection Journal

- **Objective**: To keep an ongoing record of your thoughts and feelings about autonomy and intimacy.
- **Instructions**:
- Keep a journal for one month where you note any moments where you felt a strong sense of autonomy or intimacy.
- Reflect on these entries to understand patterns.
- **Discussion**: At the end of the month, if comfortable, share some highlights with your partner and discuss.

## My Journey Through the Maze of Autonomy and Intimacy

Life has been a fascinating journey for me, and it was during my travels, meeting people from diverse cultures, that I came to appreciate the complexities of human relationships. Having lived in multiple countries and pursued various careers before settling in the Bay Area, I've been exposed to a range of attitudes toward love, commitment, and personal freedom.

I met my partner at a time when both of us were exploring our individual paths. I was deeply immersed in my studies, focusing on Counseling Psychology, while my partner was navigating the realms of their own professional and personal aspirations. At first glance, one might think that two such independently driven individuals might find it challenging to build a life together. However, it was precisely this shared value for personal autonomy that served as the cornerstone of our burgeoning relationship.

Our first year was a whirlwind of passion and exploration. While we relished the honeymoon phase, both of us consciously maintained space for personal growth. Weekends were often split between romantic getaways and solitary retreats, or sometimes professional development seminars and courses. The experience was liberating; we were two individual entities choosing to intertwine our lives while acknowledging each other's autonomy.

However, as is the case in any real relationship, the challenge of balancing autonomy with intimacy soon emerged. Work pressures for me and a family crisis for my partner led us to reevaluate the time and emotional investment we were putting into our relationship. This period highlighted the importance of the intimacy that nurtures a relationship during times of stress and uncertainty. It was no longer sufficient to maintain separate orbits that occasionally intersected; we needed to build a more robust, shared emotional space.

We entered couples therapy— a space where we could open up about our vulnerabilities and fears without judgment. This mutual act of unveiling, of seeking intimacy while preserving our individual identities, has been the most profound and enriching experience for both of us. It has enabled us to weave a tapestry that celebrates both 'me' and 'we,' enriching each thread with the unique colors we bring to our relationship.

Today, our journey continues. We've learned to savor the sweet spots that lie at the intersection of autonomy and intimacy, knowing that this delicate balance is ever-evolving. But the labyrinth seems less daunting now; we navigate it together, holding space for both individual growth and shared emotional intimacy.

## Ending Note: The Journey Ahead

As we conclude this opening chapter on the intricate dance of autonomy and intimacy in love and relationships, it's important to recognize that this is just the beginning of a lifelong journey. Finding the perfect balance between individuality and emotional closeness is an ongoing endeavor, one that requires constant reassessment, open dialogue, and, most importantly, a willingness to adapt.

If you've taken the time to engage with the exercises at the end of this chapter, give yourself a pat on the back. This proactive approach shows a commendable level of commitment—not just to your partner but also to yourself. The beauty of the intertwining forces of autonomy and intimacy is that they not only enrich our relationships but also contribute to our own personal growth and emotional well-being.

As you turn the page to delve deeper into the subsequent chapters, carry with you the insights and reflections you've gathered here. The foundational understanding of autonomy and intimacy serves as your compass for navigating the more specific yet equally complex realms of relationships that we will explore.

Remember, in the labyrinth of love, you're never walking alone. Each step taken towards fostering autonomy is a leap toward your own self-fulfillment, and every effort made to deepen intimacy is a gift to the collective journey you share with your partner.

Onward, then, to a life rich in love, balanced in being, and deeply fulfilling in its intricate, beautiful complexities.

Here's to you and the incredible journey that awaits.

# 2

# The Mirror and the Window: Knowing Yourself to Know Your Partner

Imagine standing at the intersection of two worlds—the one inside you and the one outside, represented by your partner. At this crossroads, two essential elements come into play: a mirror and a window. The mirror reflects your inner self—your hopes, fears, strengths, and vulnerabilities. The window, on the other hand, offers a view into your partner's world—their dreams, challenges, emotions, and intricacies. In any successful relationship, these two elements are not only present but also intricately linked. This chapter delves into this crucial symbiotic relationship between self-awareness (the mirror) and understanding your partner (the window). The journey towards a fulfilling relationship often begins with a step inward.

Through this chapter, we will explore advanced techniques for introspection and self-awareness and how they pave the way for deeper understanding and connection with your partner. We will delve into why mastering the art of self-reflection can make you a better listener, a more empathetic partner, and, most importantly, a more authentic individual.

This isn't just about self-improvement; it's about relationship enrichment. As you read through the pages that follow, you'll learn the value of polishing the mirror and cleaning the window. By doing so, you open the door to more meaningful interactions, more authentic love, and a partnership that can withstand the test of time and circumstance. So, let's embark on this transformative journey that begins with you but resonates through the 'us' that you're a part of.

With this enhanced lens, we will examine the mechanics of emotional intelligence, delve into advanced strategies for effective communication, and uncover the secret languages that you and your partner can develop to make your bond unbreakable. Onward to a more enlightened version of you and a more connected 'us.'

In the upcoming sections, you'll find a blend of research-backed theories, real-life anecdotes, practical exercises, and deep insights, all designed to facilitate your journey of self-discovery and relational depth. Let's turn the page and begin.

## The Importance of Self-Awareness: A Deeper Dive into Why It Matters

In an ever-changing, complex world, self-awareness stands as a beacon of stability and authenticity. At its core, it is the insightful understanding of your own inner universe—your thoughts, feelings, triggers, desires, and even your limitations. Self-awareness is not merely introspective navel-gazing; it's a tool of tremendous utility that can revolutionize your interactions with the world and, most notably, with your partner.

## The Multi-Faceted Gem of Self-Knowledge

Self-awareness is not monolithic; it's multi-faceted, much like a finely cut gemstone. Each facet—be it your beliefs, emotions, motivations, strengths, or weaknesses—contributes to a composite understanding of who you are. By polishing each of these facets through introspection and mindfulness, you not only increase your own luminescence but also become more capable of reflecting the light that comes your way. This is especially crucial in a relationship, where being a mirror and a window for each other enhances mutual understanding and deep emotional bonding.

## The Relational Alchemy of Self-Awareness

When you understand yourself more clearly, you gain a newfound ability to navigate your relationship with heightened emotional intelligence. You become better at reading emotional cues, managing conflicts, and expressing love in a language your partner can understand. Self-awareness is the magic wand that turns misunderstandings into moments of connection and arguments into opportunities for growth.

## The Virtuous Circle of Empathy and Trust

One of the most profound effects of self-awareness in a relationship is its ability to foster empathy and trust. When you comprehend your emotional triggers and patterns, you become equipped to understand your partner's. This initiates a virtuous circle wherein empathy begets trust, and trust amplifies empathy. It's a reinforcing loop that can be the cornerstone of a robust and lasting relationship.

## The Harmonic Resonance of Emotional Connectivity

When two people are self-aware, their emotional connectivity transcends mere coexistence and enters a realm of harmonic resonance. It's akin to two finely tuned instruments in an orchestra, each distinct but capable of creating an enchanting symphony when played together. This is the epitome of relational bliss—a state of being that every couple aspires to reach but few truly attain.

## Becoming an Architect of Your Own Destiny

With self-awareness, you're not just a participant in your relationship; you become an architect, actively designing and refining the shared space you inhabit with your partner. It provides you with the blueprints for understanding your needs and expectations and aligning them with your partner's, thereby creating a future that both can cherish.

By diving into the depths of self-awareness, you are taking the first crucial step toward constructing a relationship that isn't just healthy but profoundly fulfilling and enriching for both parties involved. And this journey, as with all great adventures, begins with a single step—knowing yourself to know each other better.

## The Inner Mirror: A Gateway to Authenticity and Connection

Picture your self-awareness as a pristine, reflective surface—a meticulously crafted mirror that provides a transparent view into your innermost workings. This "inner mirror" serves as more than just a reflective pane; it's a gateway to your authentic self, a self that is not adulterated by societal norms, expectations, or judgments.

## Clarity Breeds Understanding

The clarity of this inner mirror is not a given; it's an ongoing labor of love. As life throws its dust and grime, you have the choice—and the responsibility—to maintain its clarity. A clear inner mirror not only grants you better self-understanding but also unveils the authentic you to your partner. The clearer your own reflection, the more open and transparent you can be, thereby enhancing the level of genuine interaction in your relationship.

## Mirror, Mirror on the Wall

In many ways, your inner mirror reflects not only who you are but also who you could be. It reveals your ambitions, dreams, fears, and even your latent potential. This is incredibly empowering, especially in the context of a relationship. When you know who you are at your core and who you aspire to be, you can align your journey with that of your partner. You can collaborate on not just shared experiences but shared growth.

## Nurturing a Joint Reflection

What makes this metaphor even more poignant in a relationship is that your inner mirror inevitably starts to reflect a joint image—a composite of you and your partner. The deeper the relationship, the more intermingled these reflections become, eventually showcasing a symbiotic existence. This joint reflection acts as a daily reminder of your interconnected fates and fortifies the importance of maintaining the clarity of your individual inner mirrors for the betterment of the relationship as a whole.

## The Reciprocity of Genuine Engagement

By keeping your inner mirror clear and unclouded, you encourage a similar level of transparency and authenticity from your partner. It's a form of non-verbal communication, a silent agreement that both parties will strive for openness and clarity in their interactions. This creates a rewarding cycle of reciprocity where genuine engagement begets more of the same—fostering a relationship environment where both individuals can be their most authentic selves.

## A Catalyst for Meaningful Interactions

In conclusion, your inner mirror is not a static entity but a dynamic catalyst for meaningful interactions and emotional growth. The act of keeping it clean and clear serves dual purposes: it enhances your self-relationship and enriches your romantic relationship. It transforms your interactions from mere exchanges to deeply fulfilling, emotionally charged dialogues that nourish both your soul and your partnership.

By understanding the significance of this inner mirror, you are well on your way to not only enriching your own life but also deepening the emotional and spiritual bonds you share with your partner.

## Knowing Your Emotional Triggers: The Compass of Relationship Navigation

Emotional triggers are like internal alarm systems that are set off by specific events, words, or behaviors. They are deeply rooted in personal experiences, beliefs, or vulnerabilities, and their identification serves as a key to unlocking a more harmonious relationship dynamic. Grasping the nuances of what sets off these internal alarms can not only prevent misunderstandings but also pave the way for profound emotional intimacy.

## The Anatomy of Emotional Triggers

Before you can address your triggers, it's crucial to understand what they are composed of. Triggers can often be traced to past experiences, unresolved issues, or subconscious fears. When activated, they can result in myriad emotional responses ranging from irritation and anxiety to full-blown anger or sadness. Being aware of your emotional architecture allows you to navigate potential trigger points within yourself and your relationship.

## The Roadmap to Identifying Triggers

You can't manage what you don't measure. This principle applies perfectly to emotional triggers. One practical way to identify your triggers is to maintain an 'Emotional Journal.' Whenever you experience a strong emotional response, jot down the incident, the people involved, and your subsequent reaction. Over time, patterns will emerge. This practice moves you from a realm of vague understanding to concrete awareness, granting you actionable insights into your emotional landscape.

## The Power of Vulnerability: Discussing Triggers with Your Partner

One of the most transformative aspects of identifying your emotional triggers is equipping you to have meaningful dialogues with your partner. Sharing this sensitive information requires vulnerability, but it's a vulnerability that breeds trust and intimacy. When you openly communicate about your triggers, you accomplish several vital things:

- You Educate Your Partner: Knowledge is power; in this case, your partner gains the power to better understand you and what makes you tick emotionally.
- Creating a Sanctuary for Emotional Expression: Discussing triggers often involves sharing the deeper, more hidden parts of yourself, allowing for a relationship where emotional expression is valued and safe.
- Collaborative Problem-Solving: Once triggers are laid bare, they lose their potency. Together, you can develop coping strategies and proactive measures to handle these emotional landmines.

## The Ripple Effect of Self-Awareness

Understanding your emotional triggers is a powerful tool that can transform your relationship. By gaining clarity on what arouses strong emotions in you, you enable your partner to understand your emotional world more deeply, fostering a connection that transcends the physical and intellectual. This emotional bond can weather any storm and capture the winds of joy and happiness more effectively. By mastering your triggers, you not only avoid emotional pitfalls but also nourish the soil in which your relationship grows, creating a more fulfilling and enriching partnership.

## The Window: Understanding Your Partner Through the Lens of Self-Awareness

Understanding your partner starts with understanding yourself. The process is symbiotic: the more self-aware you are, the richer and more nuanced your understanding of your partner becomes. In essence, your 'inner mirror' of self-awareness and your 'window' into understanding your partner are both frames through which the complete picture of your relationship is viewed.

## The Interconnectedness of Self-Awareness and Relationship Dynamics

Consider your relationship as an intricate dance, a dynamic equilibrium. The "mirror" of self-awareness allows you to understand the steps you are taking—the pace, the rhythm, your posture—while the "window" serves as a lens through which you can anticipate your partner's moves, respond to their cues, and contribute to a harmonious performance. When you are well-aligned with your own emotions and triggers, you naturally become more attuned to your partner's emotional needs and states.

## Cultivating the Art of Empathetic Listening

We've previously discussed the importance of listening with empathy in Chapter 1. Here, we elaborate on how this practice dovetails with self-awareness to create an even more impactful communication strategy. By being aware of your own biases, emotional triggers, and response patterns, you can better bracket your own experiences to offer your partner an undiluted space of empathetic listening.

For instance, if you know you have a trigger around feeling controlled due to past experiences, you can identify when this bias is affecting your ability to genuinely hear your partner when they ask for something. Recognizing your own biases frees you to be present with your partner, enhancing the quality of your listening.

## The Emotional Alchemy of Empathy and Self-Awareness

Pairing empathy with self-awareness creates a kind of emotional alchemy. It moves you beyond a superficial understanding of your partner to a more intimate, nuanced comprehension. This goes beyond merely knowing their likes and dislikes but extends to a profound understanding of their fears, hopes, dreams, and insecurities.

Your empathetic listening, enriched by your self-awareness, allows you to catch the subtle undertones in your partner's communication, the unspoken messages, and the emotional subtext. It elevates the conversation from transactional to transformational, offering both of you a safe space for emotional expression and mutual growth.

## Building A Bridge of Mutual Understanding

The "mirror" and the "window" are not isolated; they are interconnected tools in building a bridge of mutual understanding and emotional intimacy. The self-awareness gained from looking into your 'inner mirror' arms you with the emotional intelligence needed to peer meaningfully through the 'window' into your partner's world. By harmonizing both, you lay down a strong foundation for a relationship that is not only enduring but also enriching.

# Real Life Stories

*Disclaimer: All names and identifying details have been changed to protect confidentiality. The therapist referred to is the book's author.*

## Story 1: Lisa and Peter — The Importance of Self-Awareness

Lisa and Peter came to see me after five years of marriage. They felt that their relationship had become stagnant; both felt unheard and misunderstood. During our sessions, it became clear that Lisa was struggling with self-awareness. She didn't know what she wanted in life or in her marriage, making it impossible for Peter to meet her needs or for her to meet his.

Lisa began a journey of introspection, using techniques such as journaling and mindfulness meditation. These activities served as her "mirror," helping her understand her needs, wants, and emotional triggers.

Once Lisa gained self-awareness, she became more transparent about her needs, making it easier for Peter to understand and meet them. Their communication improved, and so did their marriage.

## Story 2: Maria and Alex — Understanding Emotional Triggers

Maria and Alex, a couple in their late thirties, sought therapeutic intervention due to their recurrent arguments, which they could neither resolve nor understand. The therapy sessions facilitated a deeper exploration of their emotional triggers, which paved the way for progress.

During the therapy sessions, the couple was advised to maintain an "Emotional Journal" to identify the triggers that led to their arguments. By keeping this journal, they could document their emotional responses and understand the underlying reasons for their disagreements.

Maria realized that Alex's habit of interrupting her was triggering feelings of invalidation in her, which originated from her childhood experiences. In contrast, Alex recognized that his trigger was Maria's tendency to withdraw during conflicts, which reminded him of his previous relationship, where lack of communication was a significant issue. Acknowledging these triggers allowed them to handle their arguments more effectively, turning them into opportunities for personal growth. By recognizing and addressing their emotional triggers, they were able to develop a better understanding of each other's perspectives, navigate their arguments more effectively, and create a more harmonious and loving relationship.

## Story 3: Emily and Sarah — Empathetic Listening

Emily and Sarah sought therapy to improve their communication. Although Emily believed she was a good listener, Sarah felt otherwise.

During therapy, Emily was introduced to the "window" metaphor to practice empathetic listening. This involved setting aside her own judgments and focusing on Sarah's words and emotions. Emily realized that she had been more focused on waiting for her turn to speak rather than understanding Sarah.

With empathetic listening, Sarah felt more valued and heard, which strengthened their emotional bond.

## Story 4: Jake and Robert — The Art of Self-Expression

Jake and Robert struggled with emotional intimacy. Robert was particularly reserved and struggled to express his feelings, making Jake feel emotionally disconnected from him.

Through individual sessions focusing on the "inner mirror," Robert was encouraged to confront his fears around vulnerability and self-expression. He learned to articulate his feelings more openly, which made him feel more connected to himself and deepened his emotional connection with Jake.

Their relationship became more genuine and satisfying as they started to share more openly with each other.

These stories encapsulate how focusing on the "mirror" of self-awareness and the "window" into your partner's world can significantly improve relationship dynamics. By working on both these aspects, my clients were able to create a more enriching, satisfying partnership, proving that the journey towards a fulfilling relationship indeed begins with a step inward.

## Recommended Exercises

Exercise 1: The Inner Mirror Journal

Objective: To develop a clearer understanding of your thoughts, emotions, and triggers.

- Take a notebook and label it as your "Inner Mirror Journal."
- For a week, jot down events or interactions that sparked any strong emotional responses in you, positive or negative.
- After the week, review your entries and identify patterns or triggers.

Exercise 2: The Self-Awareness Dialogue

Objective: To openly discuss your triggers and emotional needs with your partner, thereby fostering a safe space for emotional expression.

- Set aside a time with your partner where you can have an uninterrupted conversation.
- Each partner takes turns sharing one trigger or emotional need.
- The listening partner practices active listening, refrains from interrupting, and then validates the sharing partner's feelings.
- Switch roles.

Exercise 3: The Window Walk

Objective: To learn more about your partner's world by engaging in one of their interests.

- Each partner picks an activity or interest that is particularly meaningful to them but may not be to the other.
- Spend a day engaging in these activities together.
- Discuss what you each learned about the other's world and interests after the activity.

Exercise 4: Empathic Listening Exercise

Objective: To practice empathic listening by paying close attention to your partner's verbal and non-verbal cues.

- One partner shares a minor recent event where they experienced some emotional upheaval.
- The other partner listens without interrupting, focusing not only on the words but also on body language, tone, and facial expression.
- After the sharing, the listening partner repeats what they have gathered, both the content and the emotional undertones.

Exercise 5: Self-Awareness and Partner Awareness Questionnaire

Objective: To reflect on your self-awareness and understanding of your partner.

- Both partners complete a questionnaire that includes questions like:
- What are my emotional triggers?
- How do I typically respond to stress?
- How well do I understand my partner's emotional needs?
- What are the emotional barriers I've noticed in my partner?
- Discuss your answers openly with each other.

By engaging in these exercises, you'll be taking proactive steps toward a deeper emotional connection and understanding of yourself and your partner. Remember, self-awareness and mutual understanding are ongoing processes that require regular maintenance, much like any other form of health and wellness.

## Personal Story: A Journey of Mutual Discovery

My partner and I often drifted apart into our separate worlds. While he was busy with his demanding business career, I was immersed in my clients' complex emotional struggles in my clinical practice. Though we were committed to each other, it felt like we were gazing through cloudy windows into each other's lives. Over time, the glass frosted, making it difficult to see each other clearly and truly understand the essence of each other's daily experiences and deepest feelings.

One evening, as we sat down for dinner, we could feel the emotional distance between us. Though we talked, it felt like a hollow conversation. We listened, but something vital seemed lost in translation. This moment served as our wake-up call.

As a psychotherapist who helps others become more self-aware, I realized that I had been overlooking my own emotional landscape. That's when I decided to engage in introspection, to look at what I was bringing to the relationship. This self-reflective journey was both enlightening and humbling. I discovered that I had been contributing pockets of impatience and emotional distance, and with this newfound clarity, I approached my partner.

We engaged in one of the most heartfelt and transparent conversations we've ever had. He, too, had undergone a journey of self-discovery and was eager to discuss what he had found. Cleaning our 'inner mirrors' not only helped improve our relationship but also clarified the 'windows' between our worlds. Conversations became more meaningful, and we began to understand the pressures and nuances of each other's day-to-day lives. This enriched our individual experiences of the world.

Now, we make it a priority to maintain both the 'mirror' and the 'window.' Each week, we set aside time to self-reflect and share these reflections with each other. This practice has become the cornerstone of our relationship. Though the process is ongoing and not always easy, the beauty lies in the journey itself. We may never fully clear the frost from the windows or all the smudges from the mirrors, but the constant effort to do so brings us closer than we ever imagined. Through the mirror and the window, we continually discover new emotional landscapes, both within ourselves and in each other, that we never knew existed—and that has made all the difference.

## Ending Note

The journey of understanding oneself is an ongoing and crucial process for any successful relationship. Equipping yourself with the right tools and techniques will enable you to increase your self-awareness and, in turn, understand your partner better. Self-awareness and understanding your partner's emotional landscape is a dynamic interplay that requires constant nurturing.

The exercises provided in this chapter can be a starting point, but the real beauty of self-awareness lies in its continuous unfolding and ongoing discovery that reveals not just who you are but who you can become individually and as part of a couple.

Committing to personal growth and helping each other grow is what makes relationships fulfilling. Though you may not always understand each other perfectly, the effort you put into understanding will pay off in countless ways, enriching your relationship's emotional tapestry and strengthening its foundation for years to come.

Remember that every day brings an opportunity for greater awareness and connection. Embrace it.

# 3

# Personal Spaces: Crafting and Sustaining Boundaries

Personal space isn't merely a luxury; it's a fundamental necessity for human flourishing. The dimensions of this personal space extend far beyond the physical; they encapsulate our emotional, psychological, and even digital realms. Yet, when we enter into relationships, the lines demarcating these spaces can blur, raising pivotal questions. How do we maintain our individuality while nurturing closeness? How can we love deeply without losing ourselves in the process? How do we construct boundaries without erecting walls?

In a relational context, preserving personal space is akin to an intricate dance—each step calculated but fluid, each move independent yet interconnected. Achieving this delicate balance is no small feat, but the reward is a relationship marked by mutual respect, emotional depth, and enduring intimacy.

This chapter seeks to serve as your compass, guiding you through the complexities of crafting and upholding your boundaries. It aims to equip you with the tools and insights needed to establish a relational environment where both intimacy and individuality can flourish in harmonious coexistence.

## The Unspoken Power of Personal Space

*The Indispensable Role of Boundaries and the Interplay of Mutual Respect*

Boundaries are far more than invisible demarcations that separate us from others; they are the foundational architecture of our emotional and psychological well-being. These lines are not drawn to isolate but to create a sanctuary for individual expression and self-discovery. Within the context of a relationship, the absence or neglect of such essential boundaries can rapidly devolve into emotional depletion, erosion of self-identity, and escalating conflict.

## The Symbiotic Nature of Respect

But boundaries are not just self-serving constructs. They also serve the relationship as a whole. Mutual respect is the bedrock on which any healthy relationship is built, and acknowledging each other's personal space is a significant pillar of that foundation. When both partners engage in the intentional act of recognizing and respecting each other's boundaries, it engenders a sense of security and freedom. This duality—security from knowing your limits are respected and freedom from being able to express yourself authentically—creates a fertile ground for trust, intimacy, and enduring love to flourish.

So, as we traverse the complex landscape of relational dynamics, understanding and respecting boundaries emerge not merely as a recommended practice but as an indispensable ethic. It is a two-way street of giving and receiving respect, a reciprocal relationship that elevates both individuals and the union they share.

## The Multifaceted Nature of Boundaries

*The Three Pillars: Physical, Emotional, and Digital Dimensions*

### Physical Boundaries

Physical boundaries go beyond mere spatial considerations to encapsulate the nuanced realms of bodily autonomy and personal privacy. They provide a framework for comfort zones and individual preferences in the public and private spheres. While some might revel in public displays of affection, others might find solace in more subdued, intimate settings. The physical aspect is not just an outline but a vivid tapestry that reveals how you wish to interact with the world and, more specifically, your partner.

## Emotional Boundaries

The emotional landscape of boundaries delves deep into the recesses of our psyche, including our thoughts, feelings, and past experiences. Emotional boundaries are the intangible fences that help preserve our sense of self and secure our mental and emotional well-being. They serve as a shield, safeguarding our emotional integrity and ensuring that we don't feel infringed upon or overwhelmed.

## Digital Boundaries

In our digitally interconnected age, the emergence of digital boundaries is not just timely but imperative. This sphere encompasses the choices we make around sharing or keeping private our social media accounts, text messages, and even personal data. In the virtual realm, as in the physical and emotional, boundaries define our interactions and offer a sense of control and agency.

## The Art of Crafting Boundaries

### *The Keystone of Communication*

Clarity is the cornerstone of effective boundary-setting. Without open, honest communication, any attempt to establish boundaries can devolve into guesswork and misinterpretation. Both partners must be explicit about their comfort zones, red lines, and the gray areas that warrant further discussion.

### *The Power of "I" Statements*

Utilizing "I" statements can significantly enhance a conversation about boundaries. This personalized approach allows you to convey your needs and preferences in a way that is assertive yet respectful, reducing the likelihood of defensiveness or misunderstanding from your partner.

The Lifelong Journey of Sustaining Boundaries

### *Periodic Audits*

Boundaries are not set in stone; they are fluid constructs that may evolve over time due to changing circumstances or emotional states. Regular check-ins provide an opportunity to reassess, fine-tune, and, if needed, recalibrate the boundaries that govern your relationship.

### *Navigating the Tightrope: Overcoming Challenges*

Even the best-laid boundaries are susceptible to external pressures and internal doubts. Whether these challenges come from societal norms, peer pressure, or personal insecurities, maintaining your boundaries can sometimes feel like walking a tightrope. This section offers practical advice and strategies for steadfastly upholding your boundaries, even when they're under siege.

# Real Life Stories

*Disclaimer: All names and identifying details have been changed to protect confidentiality. The therapist referred to is the book's author.*

## Story 1: Sophia and Ethan Struggle with Digital Boundaries

Sophia and Ethan came to me for counseling after two years of living together. They described their relationship as "generally good," but Sophia was bothered by the absence of digital boundaries. Ethan would often use her phone or computer without asking, arguing that they had nothing to hide from each other.

Sophia felt her personal space was being violated but couldn't articulate why it bothered her so much. After some exploration, it became clear that Sophia associated her digital life with her individuality, something she felt was getting blurred in their life together.

We worked on strategies to communicate these feelings without triggering defensiveness. Ethan initially struggled with understanding Sophia's perspective but eventually realized that boundaries were not barriers but bridges to mutual respect and trust.

They agreed to ask for permission before using each other's digital devices and set clear guidelines about sharing passwords. This compromise restored a sense of personal space and respect in their relationship.

## Story 2: Laura and David Tackle Emotional Boundaries

Laura and David were a married couple in their late 30s. Laura was a stay-at-home mom, and David was a corporate executive. David had a way of making financial decisions without consulting Laura, justifying it by saying that he was the primary breadwinner.

Laura felt marginalized and emotionally distanced due to the lack of inclusivity in major family decisions. When they came for counseling, it was evident that the absence of clear emotional boundaries was leading to resentment.

We began by exploring the underlying dynamics and beliefs that led David to assume such control. Simultaneously, Laura learned to articulate her feelings and her need for inclusion using "I" statements.

The couple agreed to set new boundaries: all major financial decisions would be discussed and agreed upon collectively, respecting each partner's role in the family. This change may seem small, but it had a profound impact on their emotional connection, leading to a more balanced and respectful relationship.

These client stories showcase the profound impact that well-negotiated boundaries can have on different aspects of a relationship. Setting and sustaining boundaries isn't just about preventing conflicts; it's about creating a framework for respectful, loving interactions.

## Recommended Exercises

1. Identify Your Boundaries

- **Activity:** Write down what you consider to be your physical, emotional, and digital boundaries.
- **Purpose:** To clearly articulate your own boundaries so that you can communicate them effectively to your partner.

2. The Boundary Discussion

- **Activity:** Set aside some time with your partner to openly discuss your boundaries.
- **Purpose:** To create a safe space for mutual understanding and respect.

3. "I" Statement Practice

- **Activity:** Write down and practice expressing your boundaries using "I" statements. For example, "I feel more focused when I have some time alone in the office."

- **Purpose:** To communicate your needs in a way that doesn't make your partner feel attacked or defensive.

4. Boundary Check-in

- **Activity:** Calendar a monthly 'Boundary Check-in' with your partner.
- **Purpose:** To review and, if necessary, adjust your boundaries as situations and feelings change.

5. The "No" Exercise

- **Activity:** For one week, practice saying "no" to small things that you would usually agree to but would rather not.
- **Purpose:** To become more comfortable with setting boundaries and recognizing that it is okay to put your own needs first sometimes.

6. Observe Digital Boundaries

- **Activity:** For a day, consciously avoid checking your partner's phone, social media, or any other personal digital space without explicit permission.
- **Purpose:** To practice respecting digital boundaries.

7. Emotional Buffer Zone

- **Activity:** Designate a 'cool-down' period after work for each partner to transition from work to home life.
- **Purpose:** To provide emotional space for each partner, enhancing the quality of time spent together later.

8. Role Reversal Exercise

- **Activity:** Spend a day pretending to be your partner, respecting what you know of their boundaries while interacting with them.
- **Purpose:** To gain a deeper understanding and appreciation for your partner's personal boundaries.

By actively participating in these exercises, you'll not only learn a lot about your own needs and limits, but you'll also become more attuned to your partner's. This mutual understanding is essential for crafting and sustaining healthy boundaries in your relationship.

## Personal Story: The Balancing Act of Personal and Shared Spaces

Living with my partner has been a journey full of lessons, especially when it comes to maintaining personal boundaries. We both have demanding careers; my days are filled with counseling sessions, research, and writing while my partner navigates the high-stakes world of business.

In the initial phase of our cohabitation, the absence of boundaries almost seemed romantic. We had a shared home office and digital devices, and our calendars were an open book to each other. However, as time went on, I started to feel like I was losing a piece of myself. There were instances when I would be engrossed in writing or preparing for a therapy session, and my partner would enter the room to discuss a business idea or share something he read online. The interruptions began affecting my focus and productivity.

That's when I realized I had to reassess what personal space meant to me, both physically and emotionally. We had an open dialogue about our individual needs. I expressed that I needed dedicated time and space for my work, and he conveyed his need for emotional availability from me, especially after particularly challenging days.

We set new ground rules. First, our home office became a "shared but reserved" space; we designated specific hours when each of us would have the office to ourselves. Next, we established digital boundaries; we no longer had free access to each other's work computers or professional email accounts. Lastly, we instituted a 'cool-down' period after work, when we could individually relax and transition from work mode to home mode before engaging in serious conversations.

Implementing these boundaries took some adjustments but made a world of difference in our relationship. A newfound respect and understanding emerged that wasn't there before. Setting these boundaries didn't create distance; it actually fostered a deeper sense of intimacy and mutual respect, strengthening our relationship.

This experience was not just an important lesson for me as a partner but also as a psychotherapist. It illuminated the importance of crafting and sustaining boundaries as a key component of a healthy, lasting relationship.

## Ending Note

As we close this chapter, it's essential to recognize that establishing and maintaining boundaries is an ongoing process. Boundaries are not set in stone; they are fluid and should evolve as you and your relationship do. The key to successful boundaries lies in open communication, mutual respect, and a willingness to compromise when necessary.

If there's one takeaway from this chapter, let it be that boundaries are not barriers meant to separate you from your partner. Instead, they are guidelines that help you to better understand yourself and each other. They serve to fortify the relationship, offering each partner the individual space needed to grow and flourish. The paradox is that by setting these individual limits, you're creating a relationship environment where intimacy can deepen and thrive.

Regularly check in on your boundaries and engage in discussions with your partner. A relationship is a two-way street, and ensuring that both of you are comfortable with the set boundaries is vital for long-term happiness and stability.

May your journey in crafting and sustaining boundaries be a rewarding one, enriching both your life and your relationship.

# Part II

# Navigating the Rocky Terrain: Challenges and Roadblocks

# 4

# The Quicksand of Over-Attachment: When Togetherness Turns Toxic

Togetherness is frequently celebrated as the gold standard of relational success—a seemingly idyllic state of being that romantic comedies and fairy tales often present as the ultimate objective. The imagery is powerful: two souls so intricately interwoven that the boundary between them blurs, creating a unified tapestry of love and mutual reliance. Yet, this rosy portrait can be deceptive. Just as quicksand lures with a surface of solid ground only to ensnare those who step onto it, an overwhelming closeness in a relationship can shift from nurturing to stifling, morphing into a form of toxic attachment that saps individuality. This chapter delves into the complex, often precarious terrain of excessive togetherness. We'll examine its insidious ways of undermining the essence of a loving relationship and provide you with actionable insights on preserving your sense of self without unraveling the bonds that hold you and your partner together.

## The Fallacy of "Two Become One": Unveiling the Romantic Myth

The poetic idea that "two become one" in a committed relationship may resonate deeply with our collective romantic imaginations. While it underscores the beautiful potential for intimacy and unity, it glosses over a critical truth—that each individual in a relationship should also stand as a whole, autonomous entity. Achieving closeness should not necessitate the dissolution of one's unique identity into a collective 'we.' Doing so can trigger a slow but sure erosion of individual selfhood, which can compromise the very core of a balanced, healthy relationship.

## Red Flags: The Symptoms of Over-Attachment

Here, vigilance is key. Some alarm bells could signify an impending crisis of over-attachment. If you find yourself unable to make even minor decisions without consulting your partner, it's time to take note. Extreme jealousy, not of others but of your partner's independent activities, is another concerning sign. The conscious avoidance of social activities, hobbies, or opportunities that don't include your significant other also fits into this worrisome pattern. These are all indicators that you might be sinking into the quicksand of excessive togetherness, and it's essential to recognize them before they escalate into more substantial issues.

## The Vicious Circle of Over-Attachment: An Insidious Journey from Innocence to Dependence

### The Subtle Onset: Innocent Beginnings, Gradual Escalation

The journey into the quicksand of over-attachment often starts on a seemingly innocent note. Perhaps it begins with a constant need to text your partner, share memes, or discuss what you had for lunch. The initial stages might seem almost romantic—the idea that you're so entwined in each other's lives that no detail is too small to share. Over time, however, these seemingly benign acts morph into something more complicated. Communication evolves into constant check-ins. Sharing becomes a necessity rather than a choice. The act of involving your partner in your life gradually escalates into a situation where you feel incomplete or anxious without their constant presence. This dynamic can lead you down a precarious path, setting the stage for emotional and sometimes even physical dependence that can take a toll on both partners.

### The Unseen Consequences: Emotional Drain and Loss of Self

As you sink deeper into this vortex of emotional reliance, the consequences begin to emerge, often subtly at first. You may notice a decline in your personal productivity, neglect of friendships outside the relationship, or even signs of emotional exhaustion. You might find your mood becoming increasingly tied to your partner's emotional state, a dangerous intertwining that can lead to volatile emotional ups and downs. Moreover, the relationship itself starts to bear the weight of this unhealthy attachment, manifesting in arguments, misunderstandings, and emotional imbalance.

## Shattering the Chains: A Roadmap to Emotional Independence

The first crucial step to reclaiming your independence is recognizing and acknowledging the cycle of over-attachment. However, awareness in itself is not a solution; it merely opens the door to actionable change. The subsequent steps involve a comprehensive approach. Setting up clear, healthy boundaries forms the backbone of this strategy. These are not merely physical limitations but extend to emotional and psychological spaces, clearly demarcating what is acceptable and what constitutes an intrusion.

Next, focus on rediscovering your personal goals. In the haze of over-attachment, individual aspirations often take a backseat. Reignite these ambitions and take proactive steps toward achieving them. Whether it's a forgotten hobby, a career milestone, or a fitness target, channeling energy into your personal goals can provide a sense of achievement and autonomy.

Finally, make a conscious effort to maintain a life outside of your relationship. Engage with friends, cultivate new interests, or even spend some time alone. A balanced, enriched life not only enhances your individual well-being but also brings a fresh dynamic into the relationship, creating a healthier, more harmonious union.

## Mastering the Art of Balancing "Me Time" and "We Time"

### The Hidden Gem of Individuality: Expanding the Scope of "Me Time"

Engaging in personal pursuits not only enriches you as an individual but also expands the reservoir of experiences, perspectives, and vitality that you bring into your relationship. More often than not, these activities act as your sanctuary, a space to rediscover yourself, understand your desires, and rejuvenate your mind and spirit. Activities such as reading, exercising, or even simple meditative practices can significantly impact your mental well-being. Having this space can make you a more patient, understanding, and empathetic partner.

Moreover, individual growth fosters self-confidence, allowing you to be a more assertive and balanced partner.

Assertiveness, in turn, nurtures open communication about your needs and boundaries, making the relationship more transparent and mutually respectful.

### Nurturing Shared Dreams: The Holistic Nature of "We Time"

While individual growth is crucial, it's not the whole picture. Relationships are a two-way street, and having shared goals and experiences is what creates a sense of mutual journey and purpose. It's the time spent together building towards something meaningful — be it traveling to new places, saving up for a shared future, or jointly tackling challenges — that adds a layer of depth and complexity to the relationship.

Shared experiences don't just strengthen the bond but also create a joint narrative, a storyline unique to your relationship. This narrative acts as the relationship's foundation, a testament to your shared history, struggles, victories, and aspirations. Such experiences are the mortar that holds the building blocks of a relationship together, adding structural integrity and value to your emotional investment in each other.

### The Symbiosis of Individual and Shared Time

The balance between "Me Time" and "We Time" is a dynamic equilibrium that requires ongoing adjustment. As your relationship evolves, you might find that your individual needs and shared goals also change. Therefore, this balancing act isn't a one-time task but an ongoing process that calls for continual attention and intentional effort from both partners.

### The Feedback Loop: How "Me Time" and "We Time" Enhance Each Other

Interestingly, the two types of time are not mutually exclusive but instead create a virtuous cycle. Time spent in personal growth activities enhances your satisfaction and functionality within the relationship. Simultaneously, the love, support, and shared experiences in your relationship often provide the emotional fuel that enables you to pursue your individual goals more effectively. It's a feedback loop that, when managed correctly, results in both a rewarding individual life and a fulfilling shared life.

In sum, the skillful balancing of "Me Time" and "We Time" is akin to orchestrating a complex piece of music. Each partner is an instrument, contributing individual notes that are beautiful on their own. Yet, it's the harmony of these individual notes, interwoven with the collective melody, that creates a musical masterpiece. The trick is continually tuning your instruments, updating your compositions, and, most importantly, enjoying the music you create together.

# Real-Life Stories

*Disclaimer: All names and identifying details have been changed to protect confidentiality. The therapist referred to is the book's author.*

## Story 1: Hannah and Tom - The Fear of Independence

Hannah came into therapy feeling lost and disconnected from herself. She had been with Tom for five years, and over time, their lives had become so entangled that Hannah felt she had no identity outside of the relationship. She had given up her hobbies and passions, constantly opting for "we time" over "me time."

Through therapy, Hannah came to realize the toxic cycle of over-attachment she was trapped in. We worked on identifying her emotional needs and set about reclaiming her personal space. Gradually, she reintroduced individual activities into her life and communicated openly with Tom about her need for space. Tom was initially resistant but started to see the positive changes in their relationship as Hannah reclaimed her individuality.

## Story 2: Michelle and Zoe - Social Media Enmeshment

Michelle and Zoe were a modern couple who took pride in their open and transparent relationship. However, Michelle began to feel uncomfortable with their lack of digital boundaries. She felt pressured to share everything online, from locations to conversations, all in the name of "keeping no secrets."

During counseling, we discussed the importance of digital boundaries and how over-attachment manifests in the virtual world. Michelle took steps to maintain separate social media lives while assuring Zoe it wasn't an act of secrecy but of individuality. Over time, Zoe came to understand, and they both appreciated their newfound space.

## Story 3: Steven and Julia - Parenting and the Loss of Self

Steven and Julia were both committed parents who had forgotten they were also a couple—and individuals. In therapy, Steven expressed feeling smothered by the constant need to coordinate every small detail of their lives around their children. They had forgotten to set aside time for themselves individually and as a couple.

Through counseling, they realized the need for boundaries, not just with each other but also in their roles as parents. We worked on creating a "couple's time" and "me time" schedule that allowed them both to unwind and rediscover their passions outside of parenting and each other.

## Recommended Exercises

Exercise 1: Self-Inventory Check.

**Objective:** To identify signs of over-attachment in your relationship.

- **Instructions:**

- List down instances where you feel you may have been excessively attached to your partner.
- Reflect on how these instances impacted your emotional well-being and your relationship.
- Discuss your findings openly with your partner.

Exercise 2: Boundary Mapping.

**Objective:** To establish clear physical, emotional, and digital boundaries.

- **Instructions:**

- Each partner gets a sheet of paper and draws three circles (for physical, emotional, and digital boundaries).
- Write down what you're comfortable with and what crosses the line in each category.
- Share your maps with each other and discuss areas where you can compromise and where you cannot.

Exercise 3: Schedule Your Week.

Objective: To balance "Me Time" and "We Time."

- **Instructions:**

- Take a weekly planner and fill in the individual activities you want to pursue.
- Then, designate times you will spend with your partner.
- Make sure to include time for discussions or date nights to keep the relationship nurtured.

Exercise 4: The No-Phone Dinner.

**Objective:** To foster real-world connection, free from digital distractions.

- **Instructions:**

- Choose a day in the week for a phone-free dinner.
- Use the time to talk openly about your day, your feelings, and anything else that fosters connection.

Exercise 5: Journaling.

**Objective:** To become more aware of your feelings and thoughts regarding attachment.

- **Instructions:**

- Maintain a journal to note down moments you felt overly attached to or when you successfully maintained a boundary.
- Review this journal once a week to track your progress and areas for improvement.

These exercises aim to create awareness and open channels of communication between you and your partner. They serve as tools to break the cycle of over-attachment, helping you reclaim your individuality without jeopardizing the relationship.

## Personal Life Story: the quicksand of over-attachment

At the beginning of my current relationship, the allure of spending every possible moment with my partner was too irresistible to overlook. It was an intoxicating period, often described as the "honeymoon phase," where we both felt as if we were becoming one single entity, inseparable and completely entwined.

At first, it seemed romantic. We texted all day and shared every detail of our lives, and our calendars were filled with joint activities. We even had our favorite shows that we would only watch together; the thought of watching an episode alone felt like betrayal.

However, as time passed, this intense level of closeness started to feel more suffocating than comforting. I began to realize that my individuality was fading away. It reached a point where I couldn't make simple decisions without consulting my partner—what to cook, what to wear, and even what to watch on TV.

It was then that I understood the quicksand-like nature of over-attachment. What started as a comforting level of togetherness had turned into a stifling closeness that was affecting my mental well-being and sense of self.

Realizing this was a crucial first step. The next was open communication with my partner. Thankfully, we both acknowledged that the situation was untenable in the long run and that changes had to be made. We began setting boundaries, both physical and emotional. Time was allocated for individual activities, and we even set some digital boundaries, like avoiding the habit of constant texting throughout the day.

Now, the relationship feels more balanced. We still have our "We Time," but it's complemented by fulfilling "Me Time," where we both get to pursue our own interests and maintain our individuality. Breaking free from the cycle of over-attachment has not only helped me reclaim my sense of self but has also enriched our relationship, adding layers of depth and understanding that weren't there before.

Looking back, I realize the importance of balancing intimacy with individuality. Too much of one, without the other, can lead to a toxic environment. Thankfully, a little self-awareness and proactive change helped us shift from stifling togetherness to a healthier, more balanced partnership.

## Ending Note

As we close this chapter, let's pause and reflect on the intricate dance between individuality and unity in relationships. The romantic ideal of becoming "one" is, indeed, a compelling narrative. But as we've explored, togetherness can sometimes lead us into the quicksand of over-attachment, a trap that can be as damaging as it is seductive. Remember that a balanced relationship allows space for each partner to be a whole person—affirming both "Me Time" and "We Time," each of which brings its unique value to the relationship's dynamic.

This is not to say that achieving this balance is simple or static. Like the tides that ebb and flow, the equilibrium between individuality and togetherness will require ongoing attentiveness, recalibration, and, above all, open communication. Acknowledge the signs of over-attachment, actively engage in strategies to maintain your individuality, and invest in shared experiences that enrich your partnership.

Ultimately, a relationship's strength is not measured by how indistinguishable you become from your partner but by how well you complement each other while sustaining your unique selves. It is within this harmonious blend of unity and independence that love finds its most enduring, fulfilling expression.

So, as you turn the page and continue on your journey toward relational wisdom, remember that love, like life itself, thrives in balance. Keep that in mind, and you won't just escape the quicksand of over-attachment; you'll build a solid ground on which both you and your relationship can stand tall and flourish.

# 5

# Isolation Chambers: The Pitfalls of Excessive Individuality

The complexities of a romantic relationship can often be likened to a finely tuned musical orchestra. Every instrument or player contributes their unique sound, yet the ultimate aim is harmony—a melodic integration of individual parts. Imagine what would happen if each musician were so engrossed in their own performance that they disregarded the rhythm and melody of the ensemble. The result would be cacophony, not symphony.

Similarly, in the tapestry of relationship dynamics, individual threads of autonomy and mutual freedom must be woven together carefully to create a robust, beautiful whole. Previous chapters have emphasized the importance of each partner maintaining their unique identity. But what happens when the desire for individuality crosses the invisible line of balance and disrupts the very essence of partnership? What happens when 'me' time starts to encroach upon "we' time to such an extent that the relationship itself starts to unravel?

Here, I introduce the concept of "Isolation Chambers," a term that denotes the self-imposed exile that occurs when one or both partners become excessively self-focused. These are not literal chambers, of course, but rather emotional and psychological spaces where an overemphasis on individuality has led to neglect, alienation, or even emotional abandonment.

The risk with these Isolation Chambers is that they often form gradually, almost insidiously. You might not even realize you've entered one until you find yourself cut off, not just from your partner, but from the emotional nutrients that sustain a healthy relationship. And while solitude is nourishing, prolonged isolation is not.

This chapter will serve as a deep dive into this less-explored yet crucial aspect of relational dynamics. It will dissect how these Isolation Chambers come into existence, identify the red flags that signal their formation, and discuss strategies to dismantle them before they cause irreparable damage. Furthermore, case studies and real-life scenarios will be explored to offer a well-rounded perspective on this complex issue.

The goal is not to make you wary of asserting your independence within a relationship; rather, it is to guide you toward a nuanced understanding of how too much autonomy can become a pitfall. Armed with this knowledge, you'll be better equipped to create a relationship where individuality and togetherness co-exist in a harmonious balance, like a well-conducted orchestra creating a captivating symphony.

So, let's embark on this explorative journey together. We will delve into the pitfalls of excessive individuality, unmask the subtleties that can tip a relationship into emotional imbalance, and arm ourselves with the tools needed to maintain a fulfilling, emotionally connected partnership.

## The Double-Edged Sword of Autonomy

Autonomy is often celebrated as a cornerstone of individual well-being and a healthy relationship. It provides each partner the room to breathe, pursue personal goals, and maintain a sense of identity separate from the relationship. Yet, like a double-edged sword, too much of it can cut deep into the fabric of your shared life.

Excessive autonomy can inadvertently create an emotional chasm between you and your partner. It may start as small gaps in communication, little moments where you choose solitude over shared activities, or subtle shifts where individual goals precede collective aspirations. Gradually, these seemingly benign choices can accumulate into a distance that becomes increasingly difficult to bridge.

This widening gap can then give rise to multiple issues: feelings of neglect, emotional detachment, and even resentment. Neglect is often the first sign, manifesting as a sense that the relationship is no longer a priority for one or both partners. Emotional detachment follows suit, replacing what was once passionate engagement with a form of apathy. Over time, this can stifle the evolution of shared experiences, goals, and mutual interests, creating an environment where individual pursuits overshadow the vital emotional and experiential aspects that make a relationship rich and fulfilling.

So, while autonomy is a valuable asset, it must be wielded carefully and consciously. Being aware of the potential pitfalls of excessive independence can help you navigate the intricate balance between 'me' and 'we,' enabling both you and your partner to thrive individually while nourishing the relationship collectively.

## The Red Flags of Excessive Individuality

It's often the subtle, gradual changes that slip under the radar, accumulating over time until they reach a critical point. Recognizing the red flags of excessive individuality early on can help preempt significant issues in your relationship. Be vigilant for signs such as:

- **Consistent Avoidance of Shared Experiences:** If you find that you or your partner increasingly opt for solitary activities over those you can experience together, it may signal an imbalance.

- **Declining Investment in Mutual Goals:** When the pursuit of individual ambitions starts to overshadow mutual objectives—such as financial planning, raising a family, or even planning shared vacations—it's time to assess whether you're drifting into the realm of excessive autonomy.
- **Pronounced Lack of Emotional Availability:** Emotional availability is the cornerstone of any intimate relationship. A noticeable decrease in emotional engagement or a reluctance to share feelings, fears, or future plans may indicate that excessive individuality is creeping in.

## The Tightrope of Balance

Navigating a relationship is an intricate dance of balancing personal autonomy with collective intimacy, akin to walking a tightrope where every step needs to be measured and intentional. On one end of the spectrum lies your individuality—your need for personal space, freedom to pursue your interests, and the latitude for self-expression. On the opposite end are the foundational elements that nourish the relationship—shared experiences, mutual growth opportunities, and the emotional intimacy that fosters a deep, meaningful connection.

Recognizing the red flags of excessive individuality is not a death knell for your relationship; rather, it serves as an early warning system, a wake-up call to recalibrate the balance between 'me' and 'we.' These red flags are not merely obstacles but navigational aids that prompt you to reassess the current dynamics. They urge you to fine-tune the equilibrium, ensuring that your quest for autonomy doesn't erode the vital shared core that holds your relationship together.

Being acutely aware of these warning signs enables a proactive approach. By addressing issues before they escalate, you can reaffirm your mutual commitments, fortify the emotional bonds, and cultivate a partnership characterized by both individual fulfillment and collective harmony. This intentional balancing act, conducted with self-awareness and mutual respect, not only preserves but enriches the relationship, ensuring its longevity and vitality.

## Finding Equilibrium

The ultimate quest in any committed relationship is to craft a harmonious space where both individuals can flourish, not just as partners but also as unique beings with their own dreams, aspirations, and sensibilities. Finding this equilibrium is less a final destination than it is an ongoing journey, requiring continual reflection, dialogue, and mutual adjustment.

Regularly revisiting your relationship goals serves as a compass for this journey, providing both partners with a shared vision to strive towards. This is not a one-time conversation but a continual dialogue that evolves as you and your partner grow and change. Openly discussing mutual interests goes beyond mere pastime activities; it serves as a chance to align your energies toward shared values, thereby enriching the relationship from the inside out.

Dedicating quality time to each other is another vital component for maintaining this delicate balance. While it's essential to honor your individual spaces, it's equally important to cultivate shared experiences that reinforce your emotional connection. Whether it's a simple dinner date, a weekend getaway, or just moments of undivided attention, these pockets of 'we time' act as essential nourishment for the relationship's emotional well-being.

By consciously integrating these practices into your relationship, you craft an environment where individuality and unity co-exist, not as competing forces, but as complementary elements that enrich each other. This intricate balance, achieved through constant communication and mutual respect, results in a resilient, fulfilling partnership that stands the test of time.

## The Consequences of Emotional Isolation—The Unintended Repercussions of Venturing Too Far Into Individuality

When individuality transcends the bounds of healthy autonomy and slips into the realm of emotional isolation, the repercussions can be profoundly damaging to a relationship.

Not only do such actions cultivate a barren emotional landscape, but they also foster a growing undercurrent of loneliness, disconnection, and, ultimately, mutual resentment.

This emotional detachment does not occur in a vacuum. It gradually erodes the bedrock of trust and mutual respect that forms the foundation of any thriving relationship. And in doing so, it places an undue burden on the emotional scaffolding that holds the relationship together. As the walls of isolation grow taller, they cast longer shadows of doubt and disengagement, obscuring the warmth and intimacy that once characterized the partnership.

Over time, this emotional distance can evolve into a self-fulfilling prophecy, confirming each partner's growing sense that they are, indeed, growing apart. Such a scenario does not merely threaten the health and longevity of the relationship; it undermines the very essence of a committed partnership, which is predicated on mutual support, shared experiences, and emotional symbiosis.

This is why recognizing and addressing excessive individuality early on is so critical. It's not just a matter of emotional comfort but of relational survival, and it demands immediate and focused attention.

## Reconnecting Threads—The Art of Rekindling Emotional Bonds Through Practical Measures

The first step towards mending the emotional rift caused by excessive individuality is a mutual acknowledgment of the problem at hand. But acknowledgment alone won't suffice. What is required is a concerted effort from both partners to commit to meaningful change, thereby setting the stage for reconnection.

**Reinvestment in Shared Goals:** Start by revisiting the mutual objectives and dreams that once bonded you. Sometimes, in the chaos of life, these shared aspirations get buried under individual ambitions. Realigning yourselves with these mutual goals can serve as a potent reminder of why you chose each other in the first place, reigniting a collective sense of purpose.

**Prioritize Quality Time:** It's not just about being physically present but emotionally and mentally invested in each other. Quality time is an active engagement with your partner—free from distractions and external pressures. Whether it's a simple dinner date at home or a weekend getaway, these moments can serve as a catalyst for reconnection.

**Enhanced Communication:** Arguably the most critical aspect of any relationship, communication should not be overlooked.

Open the lines for a heart-to-heart dialogue that enables you both to express your concerns, aspirations, and emotional needs transparently. Take this time to understand what each of you feels is lacking in the relationship, and jointly develop a roadmap to reestablish the emotional intimacy that has been lost.

In essence, finding your way back to each other is a journey of recommitment and rediscovery. By taking these practical steps, you create a dynamic environment that not only values individual growth but also cherishes the unique qualities each partner brings into the relationship, thus establishing a renewed sense of balance and emotional cohesion.

# Real Life Stories

*Disclaimer: All names and identifying details have been changed to protect confidentiality. The therapist referred to is the book's author.*

## Story 1: The Case of Emily and Mark - Independence vs. Neglect

Emily and Mark, a couple in their early thirties, were both fiercely independent individuals. They met at a mountain climbing event and bonded over their love for adventure and autonomy. Initially, their similar values seemed like the perfect match. However, as time passed, Emily began to feel neglected.

Their counseling sessions revealed that Mark prioritized his individual pursuits to such an extent that he started neglecting shared experiences. While Emily also valued her independence, she felt emotionally disconnected and alone within the relationship.

Through therapy, they were able to identify the imbalance in their relationship and worked on prioritizing shared activities and goals. This not only helped Emily feel valued but also made Mark realize that a relationship requires nurturing from both parties.

## Story 2: Julia and Alex - The Wall of Emotional Unavailability

Julia came to therapy troubled by her partner Alex's emotional distance. Although they lived together and shared practical responsibilities, emotionally, they were miles apart. Alex relished his "me time" but took it to an extreme, often isolating himself in his home office for hours, even during weekends.

The therapeutic intervention helped Alex recognize that his extreme individuality was becoming emotionally isolating. They started scheduling regular "us time," and Alex made a conscious effort to be emotionally available, something he had previously overlooked.

## Story 3: Michelle and Steven - Lost in Personal Goals

Michelle and Steven were both career-oriented, busy climbing their respective corporate ladders. But Michelle felt something was missing. She loved Steven but felt like they were roommates rather than a couple.

In counseling, Steven admitted he had been so focused on his career that he had neglected their relationship. The couple decided to set mutual goals and make time for each other. Within months, the emotional distance that had crept into their relationship began to dissipate.

These stories underline the complex challenges couples face when individuality overshadows collective growth and emotional connectivity. Each couple had to recalibrate their priorities to achieve a harmonious balance between "me" and "we," highlighting that extremes at either end can be damaging. Through introspection and actionable change, they were able to foster a more balanced, emotionally enriching relationship.

## Recommended Exercises

### Exercise 1: Mutual Goal-Setting

- **Objective:** To set common objectives and shared visions for the future.
- **How to Do It:** Sit down together and write down individual goals as well as mutual goals. Discuss how you can support each other in achieving them.
- **Frequency:** Quarterly
- **Duration:** 30-60 minutes

### Exercise 2: Emotional Availability Check-in

- **Objective:** To assess the emotional climate of the relationship.

- **How to Do It:** Take turns asking each other, "How are you feeling about us right now?" Listen without interrupting and respond empathetically.
- **Frequency:** Weekly
- **Duration:** 20 minutes

**Exercise 3: Quality Time Planning**

- **Objective:** To ensure that both partners are investing in shared experiences.
- **How to Do It:** Create a monthly calendar that includes both individual activities and quality couple time. Be sure to respect these appointments as you would any other important meeting.
- **Frequency:** Monthly
- **Duration:** 30 minutes to plan; 2-3 hours for activities

**Exercise 4: The Independence-Interdependence Scale**

- **Objective:** To understand your tendencies toward autonomy or togetherness.
- **How to Do It:** On a scale of 1 to 10, rate how much autonomy and togetherness you each feel is in the relationship. Discuss any discrepancies and how you can move closer to a balanced number.

- **Frequency:** Monthly
- **Duration:** 20-30 minutes

**Exercise 5: Five Things You Appreciate**

- **Objective:** To build emotional intimacy by vocalizing your appreciation for each other.
- **How to Do It:** Take turns sharing five things you appreciate about your partner. Make sure to include both individual qualities and contributions to the relationship.
- **Frequency:** Weekly
- **Duration:** 15 minutes

**Exercise 6: The "We" Journal**

- **Objective:** To keep a living document that charts the growth and changes in your relationship.
- **How to Do It:** Keep a shared journal where you jot down significant experiences, challenges, and milestones. Review this together at the end of each month.
- **Frequency:** Ongoing; monthly reviews
- **Duration:** 5-10 minutes per entry; 30 minutes for the monthly review

These exercises aim to strike a healthy balance between individuality and partnership. They encourage introspection, communication, and mutual understanding, serving as tools to help maintain equilibrium in your relationship.

## Personal Life Story: My Journey through Isolation Chambers

In my own journey, both personally and professionally, I've had moments where the concept of "Isolation Chambers" hit strikingly close to home. When I first moved to the Bay Area, the excitement of a new environment, career, and community was invigorating, but it also became a fertile ground for withdrawing into an Isolation Chamber of my own making.

I was so focused on establishing myself professionally and helping others navigate their mental and emotional landscapes that I inadvertently started to isolate myself from my partner. My days were so packed with work and individual pursuits that our conversations became fleeting exchanges. While I considered myself self-aware, especially given my profession, I didn't notice the emotional distance that was gradually forming between us.

Soon enough, the Isolation Chamber I had unknowingly constructed started to manifest its pitfalls. Communication between my partner and me became scarce and superficial. Our once vibrant connection started to feel like a mere co-existence. Although we were sharing a home, our emotional worlds were drifting apart, miles away from each other.

When the realization finally struck, it served as a wake-up call. I had to ask myself tough questions about how my intense focus on individual pursuits was affecting our relationship. Thankfully, we were both committed to breaking down the walls of our Isolation Chambers. We began to prioritize shared experiences again, ensuring we had quality 'we' time, and most importantly, we reopened the channels of heartfelt communication.

It was a humbling experience, but it dramatically enriched not just my personal relationship but also my professional understanding of relational dynamics. This chapter, in many ways, encapsulates lessons learned the hard way—lessons that emphasize the importance of keeping the balance between 'me' and 'we.'

The Isolation Chamber is a space anyone can inadvertently enter, but stepping back into a harmonious relationship requires conscious effort and mutual commitment.

May this chapter serve as both a cautionary tale and a guide for those looking to find their way back to relational harmony.

## Ending Note

Throughout this chapter, we've examined the intricate balancing act that is required to maintain a harmonious relationship without compromising individual autonomy. We've explored the concept of "Isolation Chambers," those self-imposed emotional and psychological spaces that can form when excessive individuality goes unchecked. Like the musicians in an orchestra, we've learned that the individual and the collective must work in concert to produce a beautiful and lasting connection.

In navigating the terrain of love and commitment, awareness is our most valuable tool. Awareness of our needs and those of our partner, awareness of the shifting dynamics between autonomy and intimacy, and most crucially, awareness of when we've drifted too far from the shared center that makes a relationship robust and fulfilling. Ignorance may be bliss in some contexts, but in the realm of intimate relationships, ignorance is often the first step toward emotional disconnection and, ultimately, relational dissolution.

Finding the right equilibrium between individuality and collective unity requires continual effort and intentionality from both partners. It's a dance of perpetual recalibration, where missteps are inevitable but not irreversible. What matters is the shared commitment to the dance itself—to keep stepping, twirling, and, when necessary, pausing to find the rhythm once again.

If you find yourself or your relationship veering toward the pitfalls of excessive individuality, let this chapter serve as a signpost. Return to it when you need a reminder or a tool to help reorient you and your partner towards a healthier, more balanced connection. The journey of maintaining a fulfilling relationship is ongoing, but it is one of the most rewarding when traveling together.

As we close this chapter, I invite you to reflect on the strategies and insights discussed. Hold them close as you continue your relational journey, using them as a guide to avoid the perils of excessive individuality. It's my hope that this chapter will contribute to your ongoing endeavor to forge a relationship where both individuality and unity are not just surviving but thriving.

Onward to a relationship that harmoniously blends 'me' and 'we,' creating a symphony of love, respect, and mutual growth.

Thank you for walking this path with me; let's continue the journey together.

# 6

# Emotional Resilience: Your Relationship's Safety Net

## A Comprehensive Framework for Unyielding Relationship Longevity and Fulfillment

Sailing through the intricate ocean of human emotions can often feel like navigating an enigmatic, ever-changing seascape. In relationships, this ocean's temperament varies—sometimes, it's tranquil, inviting, and supportive; at other times, it's volatile, posing storms and rough waves that test the strongest of bonds. Like experienced navigators who can't alter the weather but can adapt their course, what we have within our control is our response to the emotional ebbs and flows that invariably characterize our interpersonal relationships. This is where the role of emotional resilience comes into stark focus. It isn't merely a contemporary buzzword or a psychological frill; it's a foundational cornerstone that functions as a built-in safety net, safeguarding relationships by preventing minor disagreements from mushrooming into serious, potentially irrevocable crises.

In this richly textured chapter, we don't just tiptoe around the periphery of emotional resilience; we dive headlong into its layered complexities. We dismantle its multifaceted architecture—comprising elements like emotional intelligence, nuanced communication strategies, adaptive coping mechanisms, and an overarching sense of mutual respect—and reconstruct it into digestible, actionable segments. Consider this chapter a comprehensive, all-encompassing manual that not only defines emotional resilience but also explains its pivotal role in the ecological balance of your relationship's emotional landscape.

Emotional resilience transcends the realm of being a singular skill set or an individualistic trait; it's a collaborative fortitude interwoven into the relationship's very fabric. This interactive medley of skills, attitudes, and emotional literacy serves multiple functions: it mitigates emotional volatility, dissolves burgeoning tension, and offers a secure base from which both partners can explore, evolve, and expand both individually and as a unit. This robust framework provides the resilience and adaptability required not just to survive but to transform emotional upheavals into launching pads for mutual growth, deeper connection, and heightened understanding.

The pragmatic strategies and insightful pointers embedded in this chapter go beyond offering cursory advice; they are robust, life-tested techniques formulated to enhance your emotional resilience toolkit. These become your trusted compass and sturdy anchor during tumultuous times, ensuring you sail through emotional storms with not just fortitude but a sense of mastery and control.

Investing in the cultivation of this reinforced layer of emotional resilience isn't merely a defensive act; it's an affirmative action that nurtures the very environment in which your relationship can thrive. By building this emotional stronghold, you're establishing a relationship capable of not just weathering the inevitable hardships but also flourishing amidst them. Equipped with this intricate understanding and a well-stocked arsenal of practical tools, you'll find that you're not merely navigating the challenging waters of emotional dynamics—you're mastering them. This mastery creates new avenues in your relationship, wherein emotional resilience serves not just as a safety mechanism but as a powerful catapult towards greater intimacy, comprehensive understanding, and a lifetime of enduring, enriching love.

## Navigating the Multifaceted Realm of Emotional Resilience: An Expansive Mosaic of Psychological Facets

Emotional resilience is neither a fleeting buzzword nor a singular trait; it's a nuanced, multi-layered mosaic crafted from a diverse range of psychological elements. Picture this elaborate composition as a sophisticated puzzle where each piece—ranging from coping mechanisms, emotional intelligence, and advanced communication abilities to life-acquired wisdom—holds unique yet interconnected importance. Envision this mosaic as a dynamically evolving creation where each tile represents an invaluable skill, attitude, or lesson learned from the highs and lows of life's journey.

Within this rich expanse, each core element harbors its own set of intricacies. Coping mechanisms, for example, span an array of strategies, from mindfulness-based stress-reduction techniques to action-focused tactics like pragmatic problem-solving. Emotional intelligence itself is a multi-pronged construct, encompassing not just self-awareness but also keen empathetic skills, the art of reading emotional undercurrents, and the capacity for constructive emotional responsiveness.

Communication proficiency transcends mere verbal expression; it encapsulates the essence of active listening, clear and compassionate articulation, and mastery over non-verbal signals, including facial expressions, eye contact, and tactile cues. The wisdom accrued from life's diverse experiences serves as a kind of adhesive, binding these other facets together while providing a depth of understanding that informs present decisions and attitudes in a profoundly enlightened way.

When it comes to romantic relationships, this comprehensive mosaic becomes nothing short of vital. Relationships are emotionally intense landscapes, rich terrains where the spectrum of human emotion—from joy and passion to anger and jealousy—manifests in its full glory. In this ever-shifting emotional environment, the mosaic of emotional resilience functions as your safety harness. It offers a stabilizing counterweight that prevents minor quarrels from spiraling into major disputes and transmutes significant conflicts into stepping stones for mutual growth and deeper understanding.

Investing in the fortification of each element in your emotional mosaic is akin to building an emotional sanctuary. This sanctuary is a haven that not only safeguards but also elevates your relationship. Each reinforced element within this sanctuary stands as a monument to a particular facet of resilience, whether that be patience, understanding, compassion, or a commitment to common goals and values.

Therefore, as you traverse the labyrinthine pathways of love, romance, and long-term commitment, bear in mind that cultivating emotional resilience is a continuous endeavor. It's an ever-evolving, dynamic process demanding unceasing vigilance, adaptation, and cooperative input from both partners. By investing in this ongoing process, you're not merely prolonging the lifespan of your relationship; you're enriching its quality, fortifying its strength, and priming it to effectively handle whatever highs and lows the future may hold.

## The Architecture of Resilient Relationships: Mastering the Four Cornerstones of Emotional Fortitude

A resilient relationship doesn't merely happen; it's consciously built and meticulously maintained like an architectural masterpiece. Picture it as a grand citadel, anchored by four towering pillars that stand tall against both the internal and external pressures that life throws its way. These four pillars—Open Communication, Flexibility, Mutual Respect, and Shared Problem-Solving—serve as both the foundation and fortification of any emotionally resilient partnership. Let's delve into the nuanced characteristics of these foundational elements:

- **Open Communication: The Safe Haven of Emotional Exchange**

In the stronghold of a resilient relationship, open communication functions as a refuge—a hallowed space where both partners can lay bare their hopes, fears, vulnerabilities, and dreams, assured of an empathetic ear and compassionate response. This goes beyond simply relaying thoughts or day-to-day experiences; it includes sharing the core of one's emotional landscape with the comforting expectation that your partner will reciprocate with authentic understanding and compassionate engagement.

- **Flexibility: The Living, Breathing Connective Tissue**

In a world where change is the only constant, rigidity can be the Achilles heel that weakens the structure of a relationship. Flexibility, then, is the connective tissue that keeps the partnership supple and robust. It encourages both partners to be adaptable and responsive to life's many unforeseen twists and turns, viewing challenges not as dire threats but as opportunities for collective learning and growth.

- **Mutual Respect: The Unbreakable Covenant**

Transcending mere politeness or routine admiration, mutual respect in the context of a resilient relationship is akin to a sacred covenant. It's an unwavering commitment that each partner will honor the other's individuality, give earnest consideration to opposing viewpoints, and consistently display a level of decorum that signals deep, ingrained respect. This covenantal level of respect serves as an effective antidote to the toxic influence of contempt, one of the most corrosive elements that can invade a relationship.

- **Shared Problem-Solving: The Synergistic Engine of Growth**

When life's obstacles appear on the horizon, resilient couples don't scatter to opposite corners of their emotional ring. Instead, they come together in a collaborative dance of shared problem-solving. Each partner brings their unique skills, perspectives, and insights to the table, creating a synergistic force that propels them toward solutions that neither could have conceived alone. This collaborative spirit not only solves immediate issues but amplifies the couple's collective ability to tackle future challenges.

By deeply grasping and diligently applying these core tenets, you endow your relationship with a resilient framework capable of absorbing shocks and stressors. This resilient structure acts not just as a defensive wall but as a launching pad, propelling your partnership beyond mere survival into a realm of sustained flourishing and mutual enrichment.

## Guide to Building Emotional Resilience: A Relationship's Ultimate Defense System

The art of maintaining a relationship is akin to crafting an intricate tapestry made up of interwoven threads of emotional intelligence, compassionate understanding, and unwavering resilience. This section serves as your complete roadmap, a comprehensive guide that delves deeper into each individual tool you'll need in your emotional resilience toolkit. Equip yourself with these advanced techniques and practices to transform your relationship into an impregnable fortress capable of weathering any emotional storm:

## The Zen of Mindfulness: Your Relationship's Emotional Anchor

Mindfulness extends beyond a contemporary wellness trend; it's an ancient practice honed over centuries to create emotional stability. By deliberately focusing on the present moment, you not only disrupt the cycle of reactive emotional outbursts but also create a space where meaningful conversation can blossom. Employ mindfulness apps or guided meditations to maintain your emotional compass during turbulent times.

## Nuanced Communication: The High Diplomacy of Love

Efficient communication operates on several layers, blending verbal and non-verbal cues to foster an atmosphere of mutual respect and empathy. Techniques such as 'Reflective Listening' and employing 'Non-Accusatory Language' turn potentially explosive interactions into opportunities for profound emotional bonding. Mastering this art turns every discussion into a channel for deeper understanding and emotional healing.

## Self-Compassion: A Protective Shield for Both Partners

Exercising self-compassion goes beyond mere self-care; it's akin to creating a psychological barrier that guards against the corrosive impacts of negative self-talk and unwarranted criticism. By incorporating self-compassion exercises, you're not only safeguarding your emotional well-being but also modeling healthy emotional boundaries for your partner.

## The Diplomacy of Conflict Resolution: Orchestrating Peaceful Co-existence

Conflict in a relationship is inevitable, but it need not lead to emotional chaos. Employ advanced conflict resolution strategies like 'Collaborative Problem-Solving' and 'Perspective-Sharing Rituals' to transform contentious issues into collaborative projects. These strategies serve as the mutually agreed-upon peace accords that guide your relationship through treacherous emotional territory es.

## The Emotional First Aid Kit: Quick-Response Tools for Relationship Emergencies

Every relationship has its flashpoints. Having a set of immediate, effective responses can mean the difference between a minor emotional scrape and a full-blown relational crisis. Pre-agreed' Cooling-Off Signals,' instant mood lifters like your favorite soothing music playlist, or an 'Emergency

Gratitude Journal' can serve as quick-response tools when emotional tectonics shift.

By wholeheartedly embracing and skillfully weaving these multi-dimensional tools into the fabric of your relationship, you are not just constructing a shield; you're laying the groundwork for an emotional sanctuary. This all-encompassing approach transcends mere crisis management, elevating your dynamic to the realm of proactive emotional enrichment. You're not merely fortifying against challenges; you're converting them into stepping stones for shared growth and joyous triumphs.

Within the intricate tapestry of relational resilience, each strategy and technique you adopt contributes its unique depth and color. As you continue to fill your emotional toolkit, it's crucial to remember that these aren't just isolated tactics; they are foundational components of a vibrant emotional ecosystem. This ecosystem nourishes not just the relationship itself but also the individual souls within it. Your journey is one of mutual discovery, an unfolding exploration that continually enriches your collective emotional understanding. So go ahead—dive deep, navigate the complexities of each other's emotional worlds, and savor the deeply rewarding process of strengthening your emotional bond. Here's to building a relationship that not only withstands the test of time but thrives and flourishes throughout it.

# Real Life Stories

*Disclaimer: All names and identifying details have been changed to protect confidentiality. The therapist referred to is the book's author.*

## Story 1: Emily and Alex - The Power of Mindfulness

Emily and Alex entered therapy with me due to persistent arguments that seemed to erupt over trivial issues. In our sessions, they learned mindfulness techniques, which they decided to integrate into their daily lives. When another disagreement flared up, Emily paused, took deep breaths, and began to practice mindfulness. This pause offered Alex the same opportunity. The argument morphed into a constructive dialogue, proving the transformational power of mindfulness in their relationship.

## Story 2: Josh and Kevin - Mastering Nuanced Communication

Josh and Kevin prided themselves on their brutal honesty, but their 'straightforwardness' often led to hurtful, unproductive conversations. During their time in therapy, they learned about 'Reflective Listening' and the concept of 'Non-Accusatory Language.' Applying these techniques drastically improved the quality of their discussions, fostering understanding rather than resentment.

### Story 3: Hannah and Sofia - Self-Compassion As a Shared Value

Hannah and Sofia sought therapy with me due to increasing emotional detachment fueled by their demanding jobs. In therapy sessions, they learned and practiced self-compassion exercises, which they began to implement. As a result, they were better able to differentiate between external stress and relationship issues, leading to a more balanced emotional life and a happier relationship.

### Story 4: Raj and Aisha - Orchestrating Conflict Resolution

Raj and Aisha had differing parenting styles, a subject that caused constant tension in their relationship. Through our therapy sessions, they learned the art of 'Collaborative Problem-Solving,' allowing them to arrive at a middle ground that honored both their perspectives. This approach has since brought harmony and resilience into their family dynamic.

### Story 5: Claire and Michelle - The Emotional First Aid Kit

Claire and Michelle came to me during a period of significant family upheaval. In therapy, they created an 'Emergency Gratitude Journal,' a quick go-to strategy to find perspective during emotionally charged moments. This journal has since become an invaluable tool for maintaining their emotional equilibrium.

Through the application of the strategies and coping mechanisms outlined in therapy, each of these couples has added a layer of emotional resilience to their relationship. This not only helped them manage existing issues but also equipped them with the tools necessary for navigating future challenges.

## Recommended Exercises

### Exercise 1: Mindfulness Breathing Exercise

Set aside 5 minutes with your partner to practice deep, mindful breathing. Sit across from each other and synchronize your breaths, inhaling and exhaling slowly. Use this time to be present, clearing your mind and focusing solely on your breaths.

**Exercise 2: Reflective Listening Practice**

Take turns discussing an issue or concern within the relationship. The listener should aim to reflect back on what they have heard without interruption or judgment. This helps both parties feel heard and understood, improving communication and building emotional resilience.

**Exercise 3: Gratitude Journal**

Keep a shared journal where you both write down one thing that you're grateful for each day. In times of emotional strain, revisit the journal to gain perspective and remind yourself of the positive aspects of your relationship.

**Exercise 4: Non-Accusatory Language Role-Play**

Role-play a scenario where there is a disagreement, but practice using non-accusatory language. For instance, instead of saying, "You never listen to me," try, "I feel unheard when you interrupt me." Evaluate the difference in emotional response and mutual understanding when non-accusatory language is used.

**Exercise 5: The Emotional First Aid Kit**

Create a physical or digital 'emotional first aid kit.' Include soothing music, inspirational quotes, fond memories, or even a small object that brings you comfort. Access this kit during times of emotional turbulence.

**Exercise 6: Collaborative Problem-Solving Worksheet**

Sit down together and write out an issue that has caused tension. Then, brainstorm potential solutions, making sure to include ideas from both parties. Finally, agree on a mutually beneficial solution and outline the steps needed to achieve it.

**Exercise 7: Mutual Goals Mapping**

Create a 'mind map' of your relationship goals. Have a column for individual goals and another for mutual goals. Discuss how to allocate time and resources for these goals and how they align with your relationship's long-term plans.

**Exercise 8: Self-Compassion Mantras**

Develop a series of self-compassion mantras such as "I am enough" or "I accept myself unconditionally." Repeat these mantras individually or together during emotionally taxing moments to center yourselves.

**Exercise 9: Emotional Check-ins**

Schedule regular emotional check-ins with your partner. Discuss openly how you're feeling, any stressors affecting you, and how your partner can support you and vice versa.

These exercises, designed to build emotional resilience, will give you and your partner practical tools to navigate the emotional landscape of your relationship. Like any skill, emotional resilience takes time and practice to develop but is invaluable for creating a lasting, healthy relationship.

## Personal Life Story: Transformative Power of Emotional Resilience

As a couples therapist, I have had the unique opportunity to delve deep into the emotional complexities that both challenge and enrich relationships. Across diverse backgrounds and varying life circumstances, I have observed that emotional resilience often serves as the linchpin that holds relationships together. It's the safety net that catches us when we stumble, the buffer that absorbs the shocks life inevitably delivers.

My journey toward understanding the value of emotional resilience was not merely academic; it was deeply personal. Early in my career, I found myself struggling to balance the demands of work with my own relationship. Juggling multiple roles—therapist, author, partner—became a test of my own emotional resilience. I realized that the advice I was dispensing in my practice needed to be implemented in my own life.

There was a particularly challenging period where professional obligations clashed with personal needs. My partner and I were experiencing what I often describe to my clients as a 'crisis point.' It was then that the methodologies and coping strategies I advocate became more than just professional tools; they became survival mechanisms for my relationship. Practicing open communication, exercising flexibility in the face of conflicting schedules, and maintaining mutual respect even when tensions ran high—these became more than just words. They were actions that my partner and I consciously chose to adopt.

We sat down and devised a shared problem-solving strategy, recognizing that blaming each other would serve no purpose. This period served as a practical test of our emotional resilience, and it forced us to enhance our own mechanisms for coping with stress and conflict. It also offered me a renewed sense of empathy for my clients. The experience provided first-hand evidence of the struggles many couples face and the crucial role that emotional resilience plays in overcoming them.

Now, when I discuss emotional resilience with my clients, I do so with a deep-seated conviction of its transformative power. It's not just theoretical for me; it's lived experience. I share my own story not as a cautionary tale but as a testament to the strength and adaptability that emotional resilience can provide. It's not a quick fix; it's a lifelong commitment to emotional growth and mutual support. And from personal experience, I can attest that it's worth every bit of the effort.

## Ending Note

In the unfolding narrative of your relationship, emotional resilience serves as both the subplot and the cornerstone. This chapter has been an illuminating voyage through the multifaceted world of emotional resilience, equipping you with actionable tools and insights that will not just serve as your relationship's safety net but also as its growth catalyst.

This isn't about arming yourself for emotional warfare but preparing for a journey of emotional symbiosis. It's about developing an internal dialogue that's just as compassionate and understanding as the one you share with your partner.

In the end, resilience isn't merely a reactionary mechanism; it's a proactive lifestyle choice. It's an ongoing dialogue between your past and future selves, mediated by the actions and decisions you make in the present. It is in this dialogue that emotional resilience finds its true essence. As we navigate through life's intricate labyrinth, we'll undoubtedly encounter challenges that test our emotional fiber. However, fortified with the resilient skills you've acquired, these tests become less like impassable roadblocks and more like milestones marking your journey's progress.

In the context of a relationship, each partner's individual resilience isn't just a personal asset; it's a collective treasure. Remember, your relationship is a vibrant entity unto itself, nurtured and sustained by the emotional contributions of both partners. Your emotional resilience, then, serves as the bedrock on which this entity thrives, safeguarding it against the inevitable trials of life and enriching it in the glorious times of joy.

So, as we close this chapter, let the resonance of these lessons settle deeply into your emotional schema. Internalize them as both a safeguard and a stepping stone, as both an anchor and a sail when future challenges arise—as they most certainly will—look to your fortified emotional resilience as your guide, your solace, and your inspiration. Here's to a more resilient you and a more resilient 'us.'

I hope this closing note encapsulates the essence and importance of emotional resilience in relationships as you intended. Feel free to make any adjustments or let me know if you'd like further refinements.

# Part III

# The Art of Relational Communication

# 7

# Decoding the Language of Love: Expressing Needs and Desires

Communication is the intricate vascular system of a relationship, pulsating with the vital components of understanding, empathy, and trust through its complex network. While we often intuitively grasp its importance, the mastery of clear and effective communication frequently escapes us. This elusive skill set leaves many couples navigating a murky emotional landscape, where misunderstandings fester and unmet needs go unarticulated. As a result, feelings of isolation and dissatisfaction seep into the relationship, undermining its very foundation.

The intent of this chapter goes beyond merely shining a light on the subtle art of romantic conversation. It aims to offer you an all-encompassing toolkit that empowers you to dismantle communicative barriers brick by brick. By doing so, you'll be equipped to connect on a profoundly authentic level with your partner, thereby enriching the emotional fabric of your relationship. Through a combination of strategies, real-world examples, and practical exercises, you'll acquire the skills not only to speak but also to listen with the kind of clarity and empathy that can transform your romantic life.

## The Symphony of Verbal and Nonverbal Language

In the world of romantic partnerships, effective communication resembles a finely orchestrated symphony, where every instrument must be in tune for the music to reach its full, transformative potential. This symphony is not solely comprised of spoken words—indeed, that would be akin to an orchestra solely made up of woodwinds, neglecting the rich contributions of strings, brass, and percussion. Nonverbal elements such as body language, facial expressions, tone of voice, and even the pause between words are indispensable in creating a harmonious dialogue. Add to that the context within which conversations take place—the setting, the timing, and the emotional climate—and you've got a fully orchestrated communicative exchange.

Ignoring these nonverbal cues is tantamount to sidelining half of your orchestra, resulting in a discordant performance that falls far short of true emotional resonance. This dissonance doesn't merely make for uncomfortable moments; it can lead to a cascade of misunderstandings that reverberate through your relationship, creating tension and fostering resentment. Therefore, acknowledging and mastering the subtle yet powerful elements of nonverbal communication becomes not just an asset but a necessity for maintaining a loving, mutually respectful relationship. This section aims to deepen your understanding of these nonverbal cues and offer strategies for incorporating them into your daily interactions to create a more harmonious emotional symphony with your partner.

## The Mosaic of Individual Communication Styles

Each person's communication style is like a unique mosaic of experiences, aspirations, and idiosyncrasies. It's not a haphazard assembly but a carefully crafted pattern that is shaped by various factors, including upbringing, cultural background, past relationships, and personality traits. This intricate and complex pattern is both an asset and a challenge when navigating the maze of romantic interactions.

Understanding your own communication style is like knowing the brushstrokes that make up your half of the relationship portrait. Are your strokes bold and direct, or are they more subtle and layered? Do you express your needs explicitly, or do you rely on hints and cues? These are important considerations that can help you become a more adept communicator.

In the same way, recognizing and appreciating your partner's unique communication style is essential for understanding their half of the relational portrait. Are they verbose and expressive or more contemplative and reserved?

Do they prefer direct confrontation or lean towards avoidance and passive aggression?

When you take the time to understand these intricacies, you develop a deep respect for your partner's way of interacting. It's through this mutual recognition and respect that effective heart-to-heart communication can flourish. This section aims to provide insights into identifying these individual styles and offers practical guidance on how to mesh them seamlessly to enhance not just understanding but also emotional intimacy.

## Overcoming Emotional and Psychological Barriers

Communication within a relationship is not just about exchanging words but rather a complex dance that navigates through a landscape filled with emotional and psychological barriers. These obstacles can come in various forms, such as towering walls of pride, deep moats of fear and vulnerability, or the maze-like entanglements of past traumas. They can hinder meaningful dialogue and breed misunderstandings, making them invisible yet formidable impediments to genuine intimacy and connection.

Identifying these roadblocks is akin to mapping out a battlefield of emotional engagement. Do you find it challenging to be open because you fear rejection? Do you withhold your genuine feelings to maintain an illusion of control? Perhaps past experiences have conditioned you to be overly defensive and ready to erect walls at the slightest hint of criticism or conflict.

Once you're aware of these barriers, the process of dismantling them can begin. It is a careful, delicate process that often involves introspection, empathy, and, at times, guidance from therapists or counselors. The goal is to break down these obstacles brick by brick, replacing them with bridges of trust and tunnels of mutual understanding. This journey is seldom quick or easy, but the reward—a more transparent, fulfilling, and emotionally rich relationship—is well worth the effort.

The sections below offer a variety of strategies, from mindfulness exercises to practical communication skills, which can help you tear down these barriers and pave the way for effective and fulfilling conversations.

## Strategies for Transformational Communication

Communication is much more than just a practical exchange of information; it's an art form that, when mastered, can elevate the quality and depth of your relationships. This transformative communication involves several key strategies, each providing its unique benefits. In this article, we will explore four fundamental techniques that make up the foundations of effective dialogue within relationships.

- **The Art of Active Listening:** Listening is often a passive act, but active listening elevates it to an interactive engagement. This approach involves more than just hearing the words spoken; it demands that you tune into the emotional subtext, nuances, and unspoken sentiments that accompany the language. It's about providing undivided attention, offering validating nods or verbal cues, and holding space for your partner to express themselves fully.

- **The Wisdom of I-Statements:** Being able to articulate your own needs and feelings is critical, but the way you express them can be the difference between constructive dialogue and heated conflict. I-Statements allow you to frame your feelings, thoughts, and needs from your own perspective, reducing the likelihood of your partner becoming defensive. Instead of saying, "You make me feel...," try "I feel... when this happens."

- **Scheduled Emotional Inventory:** While spontaneous conversations have their own charm and importance, setting aside dedicated time for deeper, emotionally charged discussions can be incredibly beneficial. These scheduled spaces serve as a sanctuary where both partners can be honest, vulnerable, and open without the distractions of daily life or the pressure of time constraints.

- **Nonviolent Communication:** This approach goes beyond merely avoiding aggressive or hurtful words; it's about adopting a form of dialogue that fosters empathy, respect, and mutual understanding. Nonviolent Communication allows you to express even challenging feelings without triggering emotional inflammation. It emphasizes observing without evaluating, focusing on needs rather than judgments, and requesting rather than demanding.

By integrating these four cornerstone techniques into your daily interactions, you equip yourself with a robust toolkit for navigating the intricate landscape of emotional and psychological barriers. These strategies will not only enhance your ability to communicate more transparently but will also pave the way for a deeper, more fulfilling relationship.

## The Critical Factor of Timing and Setting

When it comes to communication, timing and setting matter just as much as what you say. Poor timing and an unfavorable environment can turn even the most thoughtful words into a source of conflict. Think of it as creating a stage for the drama of relationship communication. Get it right, and you can ensure a constructive and meaningful conversation. Get it wrong, and even the best intentions can fall flat. So, how do you determine the appropriate timing and setting for a conversation? Here are some factors to consider.

**Reading Emotional Cues:** Tune into your partner's emotional state. Are they already stressed, distracted, or emotionally drained? If so, diving into an emotionally charged topic is like throwing a match into a pile of dry leaves.

- **Personal Vulnerabilities:** Be aware of the natural ebbs and flows in each other's daily emotional states. Some people are not morning persons, and some might be dealing with end-of-day fatigue. Understanding these patterns can help you pick a moment when both of you are more receptive.

- **Neutral Ground:** Sometimes, the location itself can be a trigger. Discussing a sensitive topic in a place fraught with negative memories or distractions may set the stage for failure. Opt for neutral territory whenever possible, where both parties can speak freely.

- **Safe Spaces:** Creating a dedicated 'safe space' for deep discussions can be a useful strategy. This could be a certain room in your house or even a favorite park where both of you feel comfortable and at ease.

- **Preparation and Forewarning:** Some conversations require groundwork. Giving your partner a heads-up about wanting to discuss something significant can allow them time to mentally and emotionally prepare, which often leads to a more productive dialogue.

- **Silent Pauses:** Never underestimate the power of silence. Often, a well-placed pause can offer room for reflection and absorption, giving both partners a moment to process what has just been said.

Every conversation we have with our loved ones is an opportunity to connect and understand one another on a deeper level. To make the most of these moments, we must consider the timing and setting of our conversations. By carefully choosing the right moment and ambiance, we can create an environment that fosters mutual understanding, emotional connection, and constructive problem-solving. When we communicate with intention and mindfulness, we open up new possibilities for growth, healing, and connection in our relationships.

# Real Life Stories

*Disclaimer: All names and identifying details have been changed to protect confidentiality. The therapist referred to is the book's author.*

## Client Story 1: Navigating Emotional Minefields

Rachel and Tom had been married for five years but found themselves stuck in a loop of arguments and silent treatments. They struggled to articulate their feelings without falling into blame and accusation. Utilizing "The Wisdom of I-Statements," a strategy introduced in our sessions, Rachel and Tom started reframing their sentences to focus on their emotions rather than pointing fingers.

"You never listen to me!" became "I feel unheard when you don't respond to what I'm saying."

By the end of a few weeks, the couple reported a significant decrease in the frequency and intensity of their arguments. They attributed this success to my guidance in the art of compassionate communication.

## Client Story 2: The Importance of Nonverbal Cues

Sophia and Emily were a young couple who were still in the honeymoon phase of their relationship. However, Emily felt suffocated and was unsure of how to express her feelings without causing hurt to Sophia. During our sessions, it was observed that Sophia had a tendency to touch and be close to Emily, while Emily seemed to subtly pull back. The nonverbal cues were recognized, and the concept of "The Symphony of Verbal and Nonverbal Language" was introduced.

Guided exercises were conducted to help Sophia pay attention to her partner's cues and provide Emily with the space she needed. As a result, Emily felt acknowledged and respected, which made her more comfortable in expressing love in ways Sophia appreciated. Both of them learned how to read and respect each other's nonverbal language, thanks to the keen observations and guidance provided.

## Client Story 3: Bridging a Cultural Gap

Amanda and Hector came from different cultural backgrounds. Amanda's upbringing was conservative, while Hector's was liberal. As a result, they experienced difficulty communicating with each other. They struggled to understand each other's values and methods of expression. During therapy sessions, they learned about "The Mosaic of Individual Communication Styles," which helped them identify the cultural factors that influenced their communication. By engaging in active listening and empathy exercises, they began to appreciate their unique communication styles as strengths rather than obstacles. They used the techniques learned during therapy sessions to bridge the cultural gap that previously divided them. As a result, the couple became increasingly open to blending their two worlds.

## Recommended Exercises

### Exercise 1: "I-Statement" Practice

**Objective:** To get comfortable expressing emotions and needs without blame.

- Sit face-to-face with your partner.
- Take turns discussing a recent minor disagreement, using only "I-Statements." (For example, "I feel _____ when _____.")
- Pay attention to your partner's reactions and modify your approach as needed.

### Exercise 2: Nonverbal Cue Awareness

**Objective:** To become more aware of nonverbal communication cues.

- Watch a movie or show together, but mute the volume.
- Try to interpret the characters' emotions and intentions purely based on nonverbal cues.
- Discuss your interpretations with your partner.

### Exercise 3: Active Listening Challenge

**Objective:** To enhance your listening skills.

- One partner shares a story or issue, speaking for about 2 minutes.
- The other partner listens attentively, avoiding any form of interruption.
- The listening partner then paraphrases what they heard to check for understanding.

### Exercise 4: Scheduled Emotional Inventory

**Objective:** To create a safe space for emotionally honest discussions.

- Set aside a regular time each week for an "emotional inventory."
- During this time, take turns sharing any unresolved feelings, worries, or needs.
- Use the skills of active listening and "I-Statements" during these sessions.

### Exercise 5: Nonviolent Communication Role-Play

**Objective:** To practice empathetic dialogue.

- Choose a past disagreement and take turns role-playing each other's position.

- The focus should be on understanding and empathy, not problem-solving.
- After the role-play, discuss how it felt to view the situation from the other's perspective.

**Exercise 6: The Mosaic of Individual Communication Styles**

**Objective:** To understand and appreciate the variety of communication styles that both you and your partner bring into the relationship. Just as a mosaic is made up of various colors and patterns to create a whole, a relationship is formed from the unique ways both individuals express themselves.

**Materials Needed:**

- Two sheets of paper for each person
- Colored markers or pencils
- A list of different communication styles (Direct, Indirect, Assertive, Passive, Aggressive, Passive-Aggressive, Analytical, Intuitive, Functional, Personal)

**Instructions:**

- **Identify Your Styles:** Both of you should individually list out the communication styles you believe you predominantly use. You can pick more than one, but try to limit it to your top three.

- **The Color Code:** Assign a color to each communication style on your list. For example, if "Direct" is one style you've chosen, you might select blue for that.
- **Draw Your Mosaic:** On a sheet of paper, draw a simple geometric shape such as a square or a circle. Inside that shape, use the colors you've assigned to fill in areas representing how often you think you use each communication style. For example, if 70% of your communication is "Direct," then 70% of your shape should be colored blue.
- **Share and Explain:** Once both of you are done, share your mosaics with each other. Take turns explaining why you've colored your shapes the way you have.
- **Identify Your Partner's Styles:** On a separate sheet, try to create a mosaic for your partner using the same list of communication styles. Use your understanding of them to allocate colors and areas.
- **Comparison and Reveal:** Share the mosaics you've created for each other. Discuss how accurate they are and where there are gaps in perception. How did your partner see you, and how did you see your partner? Are there any surprises?
- **Discuss Scenarios:** Identify recent conversations or disputes that could have been better navigated if you had

understood each other's communication mosaic beforehand.

- **Strategies for Harmonization:** Finally, discuss ways you can better harmonize your individual communication styles for a more coherent and beautiful mosaic in your relationship. Do you need to adapt some aspects of your own style or adopt a new color from your partner's palette?

These exercises are intended to build upon the principles discussed in this chapter. By completing them, you and your partner will gain a better understanding of your natural communication styles and how they influence each other.

## My Personal Journey in Mastering the Language of Love

If there's one thing I've come to understand both personally and professionally, it's that no amount of expertise can fully shield you from the complexities and vulnerabilities that come with love and communication.

*The Beginning: Navigating Unspoken Rules*

Growing up in a multicultural setting exposed me to a myriad of communication styles and implicit emotional languages. From a young age, I noticed that my family expressed love in subtle, sometimes unspoken ways—acts of service, the preparation of a favorite meal, or simply being present during times of need. While these experiences were formative, they left me somewhat unprepared for the explicit verbal communication that adult romantic relationships often require.

*The Aha Moment*

I carried these early lessons into my adult life, both in my personal relationships and my practice as a psychotherapist. It wasn't until a significant relationship in my 30s that I truly understood the gap in my communicative style. I found myself in a partnership where love was often expressed verbally and very openly—a stark contrast to my own reserved style. This difference led to misunderstandings and feelings of disconnect despite the deep love we both felt.

*The Learning Curve*

Recognizing the issue was just the first step. I had to consciously practice opening myself up to not only speak my truth but also actively listen to my partner's. Techniques such as "I-Statements" and Nonviolent Communication, which I often recommended to my clients, suddenly became tools that I had to master for my personal use. The change was arduous but enlightening.

*Emotional Inventory as Ritual*

What particularly resonated with me was the practice of 'Scheduled Emotional Inventory.' Setting aside intentional time to discuss and dissect our emotional world transformed how my partner and I related. It brought us closer than any romantic dinner or weekend getaway ever could. It was raw, it was intimate, and it was incredibly revealing.

*The Therapist Becomes the Client*

As a psychotherapist, humbling myself to the lessons I often taught was an enlightening experience. I began incorporating the insights from my personal life into my professional practice, treating communication not just as a skill but also as an art form to be honed, appreciated, and revered.

And so, the journey continues. Each day brings new challenges and opportunities to refine this ever-evolving language of love. But one thing is clear: the richer my vocabulary becomes, the deeper my connections grow—both in my personal life and my professional practice.

I hope this personal story resonates with the broader themes of Chapter 7 and adds a unique, lived perspective to the importance of effective communication in relationships.

## Ending Note: The Nuance of Unity

As we bring Chapter 7 to a close, it's important to take a moment and recognize the journey you've embarked on. The language of love is a complex lexicon crafted over time and through experiences that are both uplifting and challenging. It's a language without a dictionary, yet it is integral to our shared human experience. It is what makes us vulnerable and beautifully human.

Understanding your needs and desires, as well as those of your partner, is an ongoing process. Relationships aren't built in a day, and neither is fluent communication within them. By now, you've delved into various ways to express your deepest emotions, needs, and aspirations. You've discovered that sometimes it requires words, other times actions, and often a combination of both.

In all of this, remember that patience is your ally and openness your guide. There will be moments of eloquence and instances of utter speechlessness. Both are equally valuable in the evolving dialogue between you and your partner.

The exercises and discussions in this chapter were designed to enrich that dialogue, making it more nuanced, respectful, and genuinely reflective of who you are and what you need. It's not just about expressing your desires effectively; it's also about tuning into the often subtle signals your partner is sending you, reading between the lines, and sometimes even understanding the silence.

As you continue this journey, be prepared to rewrite, revise, and occasionally crumple up pages of your shared lexicon. But each time you do, you'll find the replacement page fits a little better than the last.

As we transition into the next chapter, take with you the tools and insights you've gained here. These skills will deepen your understanding of not just how to speak but also how to listen—how to step into your partner's world and truly hear what they are saying.

Here's to decoding and recoding the language of love as you create your own ever-expanding dictionary of the heart.

See you in Chapter 8.

# 8

# The Echo Chamber: Cultivating the Art of Active Listening and the Power of Empathy

In the intricate tapestry of romantic relationships, grand gestures of love and poetic affirmations often seize the limelight, dazzling us with their overt displays of passion and commitment. We are beguiled by cinematic kisses in the rain and serenades beneath balconies; it's as if the louder and grander the gesture, the more potent the love. However, when the spectacle fades, and the curtain falls, it's the quieter, unscripted moments that form the enduring backbone of a meaningful relationship. These are the fleeting instances of eye contact that speak a silent language, the deliberate pause to genuinely listen to your partner's words, and the tender embraces that communicate a universe of feelings in a single touch.

These quiet acts of active listening and authentic empathy often go unnoticed, hidden in the wings, while grand declarations take center stage. Yet, it is precisely within these subtle, humble gestures where the genuine connection blossoms, intimacy deepens, and emotional bonds solidify. They are the unsung heroes of relational dynamics, the building blocks of trust and mutual respect that transform an ordinary relationship into an extraordinary one.

This chapter aims to shine a spotlight on these often-overlooked aspects of interaction, elevating them to the prominence they so rightly deserve. As we navigate through the labyrinthine skills of active listening and delve into the life-altering impact of empathic understanding, you'll come away with not just theoretical concepts but practical tools and nuanced insights. These will serve as the cornerstone for constructing a lasting, emotionally rich, and fulfilling relationship.

Our objective is unambiguous: to furnish you with a comprehensive toolkit that not only enhances your ability to clearly and effectively articulate your own thoughts, feelings, experiences, and aspirations but also deepens your capacity for understanding and validating those of your partner. This balance of speaking and listening, of expressing and understanding, creates a harmonious dynamic in your relationship that serves as a bedrock for genuine emotional connection.

In doing so, you empower your relationship to transcend mere transactional interactions, moving instead into the realm of deep emotional engagement. Both partners in the relationship are not just heard but deeply understood, valued, and cherished. When both voices in a relationship resonate in this manner, the resulting harmony is both beautiful and enduring, providing a stable foundation upon which a lifetime of love can be built.

So let us embark on this transformative journey together—a journey that acknowledges the monumental power of small acts, of listening intently, and of empathizing deeply. In understanding these simple yet profound truths, we set the stage for a relationship that is not merely heard but resonated with, valued, and eternally cherished.

## The Multifaceted Craft of Active Listening: A Symphony of Sensory, Emotional, and Intellectual Engagement

Active listening is neither a passive reception of words nor a simplistic auditory exercise; it is an intricate craft that requires an amalgamation of multiple skills—sensory perception, emotional awareness, and intellectual understanding. This form of listening transcends the boundaries of mere auditory engagement, pulling you into a complex, symphonic experience that involves not just your ears but your whole being—your eyes, your mind, and most importantly, your heart.

The first movement in this symphony is that of attentive hearing. This goes beyond just registering the words that are spoken; it's about tuning into the pitch, the tone, the pace, and the volume, each of which carries its own set of emotional data. These auditory cues can offer a wealth of insight into your partner's current emotional state, ranging from their level of enthusiasm or hesitation to their underlying mood and emotions.

The second movement focuses on keen observation. While the words spoken carry their own weight, the unspoken cues—facial expressions, gestures, and body language—add nuanced layers of meaning that are equally telling. A slight frown, a clenched fist, or even a loving gaze can provide invaluable context to the spoken words, offering clues into the unvoiced thoughts and feelings that may be lying beneath the surface.

The third movement emphasizes emotional engagement. It's in this phase that you connect your emotional intelligence to the act of listening. Your ability to empathize, to feel what your partner feels, is crucial here. Empathy turns active listening into an emotionally resonant experience, enabling you to not just understand but also to relate to your partner's expressions on a deeply emotional level.

The fourth movement centers on intellectual understanding. Here, your cognitive skills come into play. Whether it's unraveling complex arguments or decoding abstract concepts, intellectual engagement ensures that you grasp not just the emotional but also the rational essence of what's being communicated. This adds a layer of depth to the conversation, allowing for a richer, more nuanced understanding of your partner's perspectives.

By integrating these multiple dimensions—sensory perception, emotional resonance, and intellectual understanding—active listening evolves into a comprehensive, multi-layered engagement. It turns a seemingly simple act of listening into a profound experience of mutual discovery and understanding. This all-encompassing form of listening ensures not just that you 'hear' your partner but that you 'get' them in the fullest sense, facilitating a level of communication that becomes the cornerstone of a deep, meaningful, and resilient relationship.

## The Reflective Mirror Technique: A Multi-Layered Framework for Fostering Validation, Clarity, and Emotional Depth

The Reflective Mirror Technique is not simply an extension of active listening but a sophisticated strategy that transforms ordinary conversations into extraordinary moments of connection. Operating as a dynamic loop of validation and clarity, this method goes well beyond the mere act of paraphrasing or summarizing what your partner has said. It encompasses a multi-layered, multi-purpose mechanism that works to validate, clarify, and deepen the conversation in real-time.

The first layer of the technique aims at validating the speaker. By actively reflecting your partner's expressions back to them, you are not just confirming that their words have landed but that their emotions have been acknowledged as well. This act alone can serve as a potent affirmation, conveying that you are not merely an observer but an active participant in the conversation. It sends a clear message: "I see you, I hear you, and what you say matters to me."

The second layer aims to establish clarity. It's here that the paraphrasing aspect comes into play. By rephrasing your partner's expressions, you create an opportunity to eliminate any possible misinterpretations or misunderstandings. You are, in effect, asking for confirmation: "Is this what you meant?" This clarifying action minimizes the risk of any emotional or intellectual distortion, making sure you both are on the same page.

The third layer introduces a transformative aspect: the power of introspection. Because the Reflective Mirror Technique often prompts the speaker to further articulate or clarify their thoughts and feelings, it can serve as a catalyst for deeper emotional and intellectual exploration. By hearing their own words mirrored back, your partner may discover new layers of meaning or even come to insights that might not have surfaced otherwise.

Finally, there is the layer of reciprocity, where the practice opens the door for a balanced emotional exchange. The act of reflecting doesn't merely benefit the person being mirrored; it provides a model of empathetic engagement, encouraging a similar level of attentive listening in return. This sets up a rhythmic, mutually supportive dialogue where both partners take turns being the speaker and the listener, each gaining depth and understanding from the other.

In sum, the Reflective Mirror Technique serves as a multifaceted tool for enhancing emotional and intellectual intimacy. It transforms the act of conversation into an empowering loop of validation, clarification, introspection, and mutual growth, elevating the overall quality and depth of the relationship.

## The Multifaceted Nature of Empathy: The Quintessential Element of Emotional Harmony and Resilience

Empathy is not a mere footnote in the emotional narrative of a relationship; it's the cornerstone upon which the entire structure stands. It's a multifaceted, multi-layered skill set that operates on both cognitive and emotional levels, serving as the underpinning force that holds the mosaic of a relationship together. To define empathy merely as 'understanding' would be to underestimate its transformative power.

At its core, empathy extends far beyond the act of understanding your partner's thoughts and feelings. It demands an emotional alchemy, where you voluntarily set aside your own viewpoints, assumptions, and preconceptions to fully immerse yourself in your partner's emotional world. It's not just a matter of understanding their feelings but feeling with them, sharing in their joys, sorrows, fears, and hopes as if they were your own.

Empathy acts as a catalyst, accelerating the deepening of emotional bonds. It amplifies the sense of intimacy, fostering a sacred emotional space where both partners feel unconditionally accepted and valued. This powerful act transcends mere intellectual acknowledgment, forging an emotional connection that is both raw and profoundly authentic.

By continuously honing your empathetic skills, you're not just enhancing your ability to connect on a deep emotional level; you're also fortifying the emotional resilience of the relationship itself. An empathetically rich environment serves as a nurturing soil in which mutual respect and emotional well-being flourish.

Through the act of empathetic engagement, you cultivate an emotionally rich and resonant relational space where both you and your partner feel deeply seen, exquisitely heard, and profoundly understood. This heightened level of empathetic interaction creates a solid foundation for a resilient, fulfilling, and harmonious partnership. It's the glue that binds you together, the salve that heals emotional wounds, and the resilient thread that weaves the intricate tapestry of your shared emotional life.

## Distinguishing Cognitive and Emotional Empathy: Twin Pillars of Relational Depth and Nuance

Empathy, often lauded as a singular quality, is, in reality, a complex composite of multiple dimensions, chiefly among them being cognitive and emotional empathy. These are not just variances in terminology; they are divergent yet synergistic facets that collectively enrich the fabric of your relationship. Cognitive empathy serves as the intellect-driven aspect, enabling you to step into your partner's psychological shoes and grasp the contours of their emotional landscape from an analytical viewpoint. It's the thinking part of empathy, the analytical lens that allows you to understand 'why' your partner feels a certain way, even if you don't necessarily 'feel' it yourself.

On the other hand, emotional empathy transcends mere understanding and invites you to viscerally experience your partner's emotions, cultivating a shared emotional tapestry that deepens intimacy. It's the feeling aspect of empathy, where you emotionally resonate with your partner, providing not just understanding but also emotional solidarity.

Understanding the nuanced interplay between these two forms of empathy can serve as a game-changer in your relationship. While cognitive empathy lays the foundation for constructive problem-solving and effective communication, emotional empathy enhances emotional bonding and fosters a sense of deep, unspoken connection. Together, these twin pillars not only support but also embellish the intricate emotional architecture that underpins a resilient, fulfilling relationship.

## Engaging in Empathy Circles: A Structured Ritual for Unveiling and Validating Authentic Emotions

The practice of Empathy Circles stands as a potent ritual for nurturing genuine, empathetic dialogue in your relationship. This method provides a structured yet adaptable blueprint that goes beyond the traditional conversation format, encouraging a heart-to-heart exchange that can profoundly affect both parties involved. Within this carefully designed framework, participants alternate between the distinct roles of speaker and listener, enabling a dynamic ebb and flow of emotional energies and facilitating a balanced communicative landscape.

The magic of this exercise lies in its equilibrium. As a speaker, you are empowered to articulate your deepest thoughts, feelings, and concerns, secure in the knowledge that your words will be met with attentive listening and open-hearted understanding. As a listener, you temporarily suspend your own narrative to fully immerse yourself in your partner's emotional universe, thereby creating a space where each individual not only feels heard but also deeply understood.

Empathy Circles not only break down barriers of miscommunication or emotional hesitance but also pave the way for a more conscious, empathic interaction. The cyclical nature of this practice, rotating between speaking and listening, ensures that both participants experience the dual satisfaction of expressing and being received, making it a powerful tool for enhancing emotional intimacy and mutual understanding.

By incorporating Empathy Circles into your relationship rituals, you usher in a transformative emotional climate, one rich in authenticity, vulnerability, and empathic resonance.

## Sympathy Versus Empathy: Exploration of Their Unique Roles and Profound Impact in Relationship Dynamics

Sympathy Versus Empathy: A Comprehensive Exploration of Their Distinct Roles and Profound Implications in Relational Dynamics

Navigating the intricate labyrinth of human emotion and interpersonal connection necessitates understanding the nuanced distinctions between 'sympathy' and 'empathy.' Far from being interchangeable terms, these represent different frequencies on the emotional spectrum, each having a unique and potent impact on the architecture of relationships. Grasping these subtleties is not merely an academic pursuit but a vital endeavor that enriches the depth, balance, and satisfaction of your relationship.

## The Facets of Sympathy: Offering Compassionate Detachment

The term 'sympathy' derives from the Greek 'sym,' meaning 'with,' and 'pathos,' meaning 'suffering,' succinctly capturing the essence of 'suffering with.' At first glance, it may seem akin to empathy, but upon closer examination, the difference becomes striking. Sympathy typically operates as an external expression of concern and compassion, manifesting in a dynamic where one person dispenses emotional support, and the other receives it. Despite its comforting presence, this mechanism can inadvertently create a hierarchical emotional structure. The sympathizer is positioned as an emotionally detached caregiver, while the receiver becomes the beneficiary of this emotional largesse. Over time, this configuration can introduce subtle inequalities and imbalances that undermine the relationship's emotional integrity.

## The Transformative Power of Empathy: Crafting Emotional Equality

Contrastingly, empathy obliterates such hierarchical limitations and paves the way for an emotional democracy. Rooted in the Greek words 'em,' signifying 'in,' and 'pathos,' denoting 'feeling,' empathy is about immersing oneself in another's emotional world. It dissolves traditional roles of 'comforter' and 'comforted' and gives birth to a symmetrical partnership anchored in mutual understanding and shared emotional experiences.

Empathy serves as an emotional balancer, recalibrating the relationship's emotional meter and ensuring a more equitably distributed emotional investment. This leveling effect fortifies the relationship, imbuing it with a resilient and enduring emotional connection.

## The Symbiosis of Sympathy and Empathy: Cultivating a Flourishing Emotional Ecosystem

By diving deep into the multifaceted dimensions of sympathy and empathy, you do more than just assimilate knowledge; you actively participate in the cultivation of your relationship's emotional ecosystem. By consciously incorporating both empathy and sympathy into your relational dynamics, you enrich its emotional terrain, ensuring that the relationship not only survives but thrives in its emotional authenticity and complexity.

This holistic understanding of sympathy and empathy serves as a sophisticated emotional compass, empowering you to sail through the tumultuous seas of emotional engagement with greater expertise, clarity, and finesse. Through this depth of understanding, you construct not just a relationship that is resilient but one that is also capable of exploring new depths of emotional intimacy and interpersonal enrichment.

## Unmasking Our Listening Filters: Dissecting the Hidden Barriers to Genuine Connection and Emotional Intimacy

The art of listening, often considered a passive act, is far from a neutral process. Instead, it's an experience that is heavily mediated by a range of personalized filters—each shaped by a complex matrix of past experiences, ingrained biases, cultural norms, and our current emotional landscape. These filters act like tinted lenses, subtly altering the hue and texture of every interaction and communication we engage in. As comforting as these filters may sometimes be—providing us with a familiar framework through which to interpret the world—they can also act as invisible barriers that stifle authentic communication and hinder emotional intimacy.

These listening filters come in various forms and complexities. For example, a past betrayal may make us overly suspicious and skeptical, causing us to interpret even innocent comments through a lens of distrust. Alternatively, cultural backgrounds that prioritize certain communication styles over others can make us deaf to the emotional subtext carried in different modes of expression. Our current emotional states, such as stress or anxiety, can also cloud our judgment and divert our focus, affecting the quality of our listening and, by extension, the integrity of our responses.

Identifying and unpacking these intricate filters are not just exercises in self-awareness but are critical steps in forging deeper, more authentic connections. When we begin to dismantle these barriers, we unlock a purer form of listening, one that allows us to engage directly with our partner's emotional core, unencumbered by preconceived notions or reactive emotional triggers. This newfound clarity can serve as a powerful catalyst for increased understanding, paving the way for a more profound level of emotional intimacy and mutual respect.

By taking the time to excavate, examine, and ultimately discard these limiting filters, you create an open channel for communication—one that's receptive to the complex emotional currents that flow between you and your partner. It's through this unfiltered mode of listening that relationships can grow, evolve, and ultimately thrive, grounded in a bedrock of genuine emotional connection and mutual understanding.

## The S.T.O.P. Technique: Your Navigational Compass for Transcending Emotional Storms and Navigating Toward Harmonious Engagement

In the tumultuous waters of emotionally charged exchanges, it's remarkably easy to get caught in the whirlpool of immediate reactions and knee-jerk responses. Here, the S.T.O.P. Technique (Stop, Think, Observe, Proceed) emerges as a guiding compass, skillfully steering you away from the hazardous shoals of misunderstanding, blame, and unintentional emotional harm. Far more than a mere "pause" button, this strategy serves as an instantaneous de-escalator of emotional tension, affording both you and your partner a crucial breathing space to recalibrate and refocus.

Let's delve into the individual elements:

- **Stop**: The inaugural move is a mindful cessation of the ongoing conversational momentum. This is the acknowledgment that persisting on the current course is a recipe for potential emotional derailment.
- **Think**: The second stage involves an introspective inventory of your emotional drivers. What feelings are propelling your responses? Are your reactions informed more by historical triggers or the present context? This mental timeout furnishes a vantage point for a clearer, more rational evaluation.
- **Observe**: Shifting gears; this phase directs your awareness toward your partner. Scrutinize their facial expressions, tone, and physical posture. Are they displaying indicators of stress, bewilderment, or defensiveness? This observational moment supplies key insights into their emotional landscape and potential motivations, thus shaping your ensuing actions.
- **Proceed**: After this intentional emotional interlude, re-enter the dialogue with a strategy based on empathy and constructive engagement. Fortified by the reflective pause, you are now better positioned to steer the conversation toward a mutually satisfying resolution that respects each person's emotional landscape and boundaries.

The S.T.O.P. Technique transcends being just a prescriptive sequence; it embodies a disciplined paradigm of self-management and relational awareness. By inserting this crucial hiatus, you gain the opportunity to recalibrate your emotional compass and re-enter the dialogue with enhanced empathy, elevated understanding, and a more nuanced strategy. This practice not only defuses the immediacy of conflicts but also nurtures a culture of conscious, empathic communication that can fortify and enrich your relationship for the long haul.

The art of active listening and the profound impact of empathy go far beyond being mere techniques for effective communication; they are, in essence, the heart and soul that animate every fulfilling relationship. These are not just rhetorical tools to be used as quick fixes in moments of discord or emotional distance. Rather, they serve as the foundational elements underpinning the grand edifice of a loving, resilient partnership.

By committing yourself to the discipline of truly listening—a practice that goes beyond the mere act of hearing to the deeper layer of full comprehension—and by imbuing every interaction with the soothing essence of empathy, you accomplish much more than resolving occasional disputes or calming temporary emotional storms. You build a sanctuary, a sacred emotional haven where each partner perpetually feels heard, unconditionally accepted, and profoundly valued. This haven is not seasonal but perennial, a durable emotional ecosystem that not only withstands but thrives across fluctuating landscapes of joy and sorrow, harmony and discord.

In this nurturing environment, individual partners don't merely exist; they flourish. They are empowered by the unshakable belief that they are seen in their full complexity, cherished for both their strengths and their vulnerabilities. As a result, the relationship itself soars to unparalleled heights of emotional intimacy and interpersonal richness.

As you assimilate the wisdom contained in this chapter into the fabric of your daily interactions, understand that you're doing more than just acquiring a set of skills. You're crafting an elaborate, intricate tapestry of emotional intelligence, mutual understanding, and deep-rooted connection. This is the tapestry—a dynamic, living entity—that will envelop your relationship in an embrace of warmth, resilience, and enduring love.

# Real Life Stories

*Disclaimer: All names and identifying details have been changed to protect confidentiality. The therapist referred to is the book's author.*

## Story 1: Sarah and Mark's Communication Breakdown

Sarah and Mark, a married couple in their late thirties, sought assistance in resolving communication issues that had developed in their relationship. Despite their initial love and commitment, they experienced a cycle of misunderstandings and disagreements.

During the sessions, the S.T.O.P. Technique (Stop, Think, Observe, Proceed) was introduced to help the couple navigate emotionally charged discussions. Additionally, they received guidance in practicing active listening skills to promote understanding rather than conflict.

As a result of several weeks of work, significant improvements were reported by both Sarah and Mark. They became more attuned to each other's needs and developed the skills necessary to communicate more effectively. The marriage was transformed into a more emotionally fulfilling partnership.

## Client Story 2: Alex's Struggle with Empathy

Alex, a successful businessperson, struggled to empathize with their partner Jamie's emotional needs. Despite their loving relationship, the lack of emotional understanding was causing a rift.

In therapy, we engaged Alex in a series of Empathy Circles. During these sessions, we practiced putting ourselves in Jamie's emotional world and explored the difference between cognitive and emotional empathy. By integrating both, we hoped to help Alex develop a more fulfilling relationship with his partner.

Over time, Alex began to display a newfound emotional intelligence that not only improved his relationship with Jamie but also had a positive impact on his professional relationship.

## Client Story 3: Rachel's Listening Filters

Rachel had a tendency to interpret her husband Ben's statements through a negative lens due to her past experiences. This filter was a significant obstacle in their relationship, leading to frequent misunderstandings.

In our sessions, Rachel learned to identify her listening filters and the prejudices that were affecting her perception. Through various exercises, Rachel learned to dismantle these filters gradually.

Rachel reported a marked improvement in her communication with Ben. She became a more attentive and empathetic listener by removing the filters that clouded her understanding. Both Rachel and Ben were grateful for the newfound clarity in their relationship.

## Recommended Exercises

### Exercise 1: Practicing the S.T.O.P. Technique

- **Objective**: To instill the S.T.O.P (Stop, Think, Observe, Proceed) Technique as a habit during emotionally charged discussions.
- **Instructions**:
- Next time you find yourself in a heated conversation, consciously invoke the S.T.O.P. technique.
- Stop speaking for a moment.
- Think about what you were going to say next.
- Observe your emotional state and your partner's body language.
- Proceed with the conversation, taking into account this new awareness.
- **Reflection**: Take note of how the conversation differed from those in which you didn't use the S.T.O.P. technique.

**Exercise 2: The Empathy Circle**

- **Objective**: To foster emotional understanding between partners or within a group.
- **Instructions**:
- Sit in a circle with your partner or family members.
- Take turns being the speaker and the listener.
- The speaker shares a feeling or experience while the listener practices active listening.
- Switch roles and repeat.
- **Reflection**: Did you notice a change in the emotional atmosphere? Did you feel more heard than usual?

**Exercise 3: Unmasking Listening Filters**

- **Objective**: To identify and challenge your own listening filters.
- **Instructions**:
- List down instances when you felt misunderstood or found it hard to understand someone else.
- Identify any preconceived notions, emotional states, or past experiences that might have acted as filters.
- **Reflection**: How do these filters affect your relationships, and what can you do to dismantle them?

**Exercise 4: Cognitive vs. Emotional Empathy Drill**

- **Objective**: To distinguish between and practice cognitive and emotional empathy.
- **Instructions**:
- With a partner, share a challenging experience you recently faced.
- First, the listener should practice cognitive empathy by articulating their understanding of the speaker's feelings.
- Then, switch to emotional empathy by sharing how the story makes them feel.
- **Reflection**: How did each type of empathy affect the emotional depth of the conversation?

**Exercise 5: Sympathy vs. Empathy Role Play**

- **Objective**: To distinguish between sympathy and empathy in real-world scenarios.
- **Instructions**:
- Role-play various scenarios where one person is going through a difficult time.
- Practice responding first with sympathy and then with empathy.
- **Reflection**: Discuss how each approach made you feel and which seemed more authentic and connecting.

These exercises provide practical experience and insights into improving your active listening and empathy skills, enriching your relationships.

## My Journey Through the Echo Chamber

The art of active listening and the power of empathy weren't skills I acquired overnight; they were honed through years of personal and professional experiences, a collection of highs and lows that guided me toward my current practice.

### The Echo Chamber of Active Listening and Empathy

Chapter 8 strikes a chord in my life narrative, particularly regarding my relationship with my partner. We've always valued open communication and emotional availability, but it took some time for us to master the nuances of active listening and true empathy.

In the beginning, like many couples, we often found ourselves engaged in conversations that were more like parallel monologues than true dialogues. Each of us was eager to express our thoughts but less attuned to deeply understanding the other's perspective. We would hear each other, but we weren't always listening—really listening.

One incident serves as a defining moment in our journey toward mastering the art of active listening and empathy. During a particularly challenging period in our relationship, we found ourselves embroiled in a tense argument. The room was emotionally charged, and our voices escalated as we each tried to assert our point of view.

It was then that we decided to apply the S.T.O.P. technique we had read about. We paused to Stop, Think, Observe, and then Proceed. This momentary interruption in our habitual reactive patterns allowed us to recalibrate. We switched gears and entered into a new mode: a mode of active listening. Instead of crafting counterarguments in our heads while the other person was speaking, we concentrated on truly understanding the underlying emotions and thoughts behind each other's words.

The shift was transformative. For the first time, we felt genuinely heard and understood by one another. We each had the emotional space to express ourselves and the

### A Multicultural Symphony

Growing up in a multicultural background was like living within a diverse symphony of languages, customs, and emotional textures. It was enchanting but also confusing. Navigating different cultural mores meant that I had to truly listen to understand the unsaid, the half-spoken words laden with cultural nuances. This early exposure to multifaceted human behavior was my initial lesson in the complexities of effective communication.

## The Challenge of Human Connection

Years later, my travels and work in multiple countries exposed me to an even broader tapestry of human experiences. I began to understand that speaking a common language didn't necessarily lead to effective communication or deeper emotional bonds. Here, I discovered the true power of empathy, of placing myself in another's shoes, not just to understand them but to feel with them. This insight was a milestone in my life, influencing my decision to pursue psychotherapy as a career.

## Learning Through Listening

In the early years of my practice, I was eager to offer solutions to mend emotional wounds. However, I soon realized that my hurried attempts to 'fix things' were often misplaced. I had been listening, but not quite how I should have been. The turning point came during a session with a couple facing relationship challenges. I noticed that the atmosphere in the room changed when I paused to truly hear them without immediately offering advice. My clients seemed to lean in, to open up more as if my genuine listening had given them the space to explore their feelings freely. This was my introduction to the transformative power of active listening.

## Empathy Circles in Practice

My fondness for empathy circles was birthed from a series of group therapies where I witnessed individuals break down their emotional walls when they felt heard and understood. This structured approach, which allowed each participant to be both the speaker and listener, seemed to work like magic. It gave me a new therapeutic tool and underscored the importance of balanced emotional exchanges in any relationship.

### The Ever-Evolving Art

Even now, as someone who helps others navigate the complex terrains of emotions and relationships, I consider myself a lifelong student of human behavior. Each client's personal interaction continues to enrich my understanding of the intricate art of listening and the transformative power of empathy. This endless pursuit of learning not only empowers my professional endeavors but also enriches my personal relationships, elevating them from good to deeply fulfilling.

I share these personal insights not as a prescriptive guide but as a testament to the transformative potential of the skills discussed in this chapter. May you, too, find the power in active listening and the strength in empathy as you journey through your unique echo chambers of human connection.

## Ending Note

As we reach the conclusion of this illuminating chapter, let us pause to absorb the profound insights and practical tools we've explored. We've ventured into the sanctity of the Echo Chamber—a metaphorical space dedicated to mastering the art of active listening and the transformative force of empathy. Here, we learned that the conversations that take place between partners are not simply exchanges of words and sentiments; they are profound dialogues that sculpt the very core of a relationship.

The tools and perspectives offered in this chapter have equipped you with the means to elevate your communication to an art form, one where every interaction becomes an opportunity for deeper connection, validation, and mutual growth. Through the mastery of active listening and the judicious application of empathy, you have gained access to a more authentic form of communication—one that not only defuses immediate conflicts but also fosters a relational climate of trust, openness, and genuine affection.

But let us not forget: mastering these skills is not a destination but a journey—a continuing process that demands practice, introspection, and a lifelong commitment to emotional excellence. As you incorporate these concepts into your daily life, you are not merely refining your communication; you are actively cultivating an emotional sanctuary. In this sanctuary, both partners find their voices amplified, their feelings honored, and their spirits nourished.

So, as you turn the final page of this chapter, envision yourself stepping into a new realm—a realm where the conversations you have do not end when the words cease but reverberate through the echoing chamber of your shared life, leaving an indelible imprint on the soul of your relationship. Let this be your guide as you continue on your shared journey, a journey made richer and more rewarding through the knowledge and wisdom you've gained.

Here's to fostering an enduring partnership, enveloped in the warm embrace of empathetic understanding and the harmonious rhythms of active listening. Onward to a love story written in the language of the heart, a narrative that celebrates not only passionate love but also compassionate love.

As we approach the end of our journey together, we will continue to build upon the strong foundation we have created so far. The final chapter will offer additional ways for you to deepen your connection, expand your emotional fluency, and enrich your relationship. Savor the wisdom you've gathered and anticipate the remarkable transformations it will bring to your future together. Rest assured that your journey toward deepening relational fulfillment is reaching its pinnacle. Keep moving forward with confidence and excitement for what lies ahead!

# Part IV

# The Sustaining Forces:

# Rituals, Experiences, and Shared Values

# 9

# Shared Threads: The Subtle Art of Weaving Rituals and Experiences that Enrich Your Relationship

Love and commitment can be likened to intricately woven tapestries crafted from countless threads of shared experiences, meaningful rituals, and reciprocal undertakings that enrich each participant's life. While the spotlight frequently falls on grandiose expressions of affection and fervent emotional conversations, it's the more discreet, routine gestures and common activities that serve as the foundational fibers fortifying the emotional and intellectual architecture of a relationship. This in-depth chapter aspires to be your go-to manual for navigating this nuanced emotional landscape. Guiding you through a transformative odyssey, you will delve into the granular nuances of these unassuming yet pivotal acts of love and shared experiences. You'll garner valuable insights into creating your own bespoke rituals and narratives, all while mastering the fine art of balancing your irreplaceable individuality with the enriching benefits of collaborative emotional intimacy.

## The Profound Philosophy of Rituals: Anchoring Love through Symbolic Acts of Daily Renewal

Rituals function as far more than a series of rote activities in the background of your lives; they operate as the emotional keystones and signposts that guide and fortify the relational journey you're both on. These aren't just mechanical tasks conducted on autopilot; they are conscious, deliberate acts that both reflect and amplify the intrinsic values and emotional bonds that hold you and your partner together.

Imagine the simple act of sharing a morning coffee on the patio. On the surface, it may appear as just another part of your daily routine. However, beneath that simplicity lies a labyrinth of emotional, psychological, and even spiritual implications. The act becomes a serene oasis of timelessness in the midst of the chaotic rush of life. It embodies a moment of pause, a mutual acknowledgment of the importance of starting the day together, thereby amplifying the sensation of shared presence and emotional alignment.

Similarly, consider the ritual of a goodnight kiss. Far from a perfunctory peck on the cheek, this seemingly small gesture carries within it the unspoken promises and commitments that strengthen your relationship. It's a symbolic closure to the day's ups and downs, a mutual surrender to vulnerability, and a renewal of your affection and commitment. It serves as both a validation of the day that has been and a hopeful prologue to the day that will be.

In both of these examples, the rituals become emotionally charged symbols; each act is imbued with a meaning that goes beyond the mere movement or words involved. They are daily affirmations and renewals of the love, trust, and mutual respect that exist between you and your partner. These rituals also offer a harmonizing rhythm, creating a sense of consistency and stability amidst the unpredictabilities of life. Each ritualistic act becomes a small but significant cornerstone, contributing to the sturdy foundation upon which your shared emotional landscape is built. In these ways, rituals transform from mundane acts into sublime expressions of your shared life narrative.

## The Fine Art of Harmonizing Individuality Within a Symphony of Shared Life

Achieving a harmonious balance between shared experiences and individual freedoms is not merely a logistical puzzle; it's an art form, a dance requiring both grace and intention. The key is to approach your shared experiences as dynamic canvases, ever-evolving and infinitely adaptable, rather than as static, unchangeable frameworks. Within this living, breathing space, each partner is free to contribute their unique colors, textures, and patterns, enriching the overall tapestry of the relationship.

Consider daily rituals and elaborate adventures alike as vibrant arenas for mutual growth and self-expression rather than as mere checkpoints or duties in the relationship timeline. They should not devolve into predictable scripts but should flourish as laboratories for experimentation, where personal tastes and unique attributes are not merely accommodated but actively encouraged and celebrated. For example, during a meticulously planned date night or an impromptu evening, the ability of each partner to inject their preferences turns the event from routine into a shared journey of discovery. One might select a movie that reflects their current mindset, while the other curates a culinary experience to align with the theme, creating an intertwined experience that honors both individuality and unity.

In constructing these collaborative experiences, you'll find that a relationship can indeed be an amplifying chamber for individuality. Rather than acting as constraints, the boundaries of a committed relationship can serve as a fertile landscape where individual dreams, quirks, and even eccentricities are given room to flourish. This is not about merely tolerating each other’s individualism; it's about valorizing it. Each partner, in being a universe unto themselves, adds new realms of possibility to the relationship, making it a space not of limitation but of limitless exploration.

By weaving individual strands into the broader fabric of shared experiences, you avoid reducing the relationship to a confining structure. Instead, it transforms into a rich, multidimensional space, ever-adapting and continually enriched by the dynamic interplay of two unique individuals. It becomes a living entity, characterized not by uniformity but by a rich diversity—a dynamic equilibrium where 'me' and 'we' don't just coexist but co-create.

So, in this delicate balance between individuality and unity, between the personal and the shared, you don't just form a relationship; you craft a symphony. It's a symphony composed of distinct yet harmonious notes, each contributing to a grand, resonant masterpiece that not only stands the test of time but continually refreshes itself, making each moment a unique, shared adventure in love and life.

The mastery of sustaining a rich and fulfilling relationship transcends the scope of grand romantic overtures and theatrical declarations of love. Indeed, it is often discovered in the intimate tapestry of everyday moments and recurring rituals, each one meticulously woven into the shared emotional fabric of your partnership. These are not mere threads but lifelines—each shared dinner, every engaging discussion over a thought-provoking book or movie, each tranquil morning spent sipping coffee in peaceful harmony—these seemingly mundane acts are the foundational stones that fortify your relationship's palace.

Every small yet deliberate shared act is like a brushstroke in an ever-evolving painting. They add not only color but texture, depth, and nuance to the tableau of your shared life. These small gestures form the lexicon of your unique love language, encapsulating shared values, mutual respect, and deep emotional understanding. They are living testaments to the depth of your commitment, subtle affirmations that serve to continually renew and reaffirm your shared emotional investment.

By mindfully crafting these rituals and shared experiences, you do more than merely maintain the relationship; you elevate it. You infuse it with resilience, imbue it with meaning, and enrich it with a sense of joint discovery and individual freedom. You convert everyday moments into sacred milestones, transmuting the ordinary into the extraordinary. These shared moments become hallowed ground, spaces where individuality and unity coalesce in perfect harmony, creating an emotional symphony that not only withstands the vicissitudes of life but thrives amidst them.

In focusing on these miniature yet monumental acts, you empower your relationship to be more than just a social or emotional construct. It metamorphoses into a living, breathing entity, an ever-expanding universe of shared dreams, joys, and sorrows. It becomes not just an aspect of your life but a dynamic, nurturing force that enriches every facet of your individual and collective being.

And so, as you venture forth into the labyrinthine journey of love and companionship, know that your ability to create and cherish these shared experiences will serve as both compass and keystone—guiding you through challenges and anchoring you in emotional depths for a relationship that is not just enduring but perpetually enchanting.

## Real-life Stories

*Disclaimer: All names and identifying details have been changed to protect confidentiality. The therapist referred to is the book's author.*

### Story 1: Ana and Carlos - "The Gratitude Journal"

Ana and Carlos came to therapy struggling with the aftermath of a traumatic event that shook their lives. While Carlos was dealing with anxiety and was hesitant to venture outside, Ana was experiencing depressive episodes. They were desperately looking for ways to reconnect emotionally.

They were introduced to the idea of a "Gratitude Journal," a daily practice where each would write down one thing they were grateful for about the other person or their relationship.

Despite their initial skepticism, they tried it out. Within a few weeks, they noticed a change. Focusing on gratitude allowed them to create a shared thread of positivity that wove its way through their daily interactions. It didn't solve all their problems, but it laid the groundwork for deeper emotional healing and mutual support.

### Story 2: Raj and Priya - "Weekly Cultural Exploration"

Raj and Priya were a multicultural couple trying to integrate their diverse backgrounds into one harmonious life. Raj was born in India, and Priya grew up in Japan. Both felt that their cultural differences were becoming a point of contention rather than a source of enrichment.

In therapy, they were encouraged to make their cultural diversity a "shared thread" in their relationship. They decided to dedicate one night a week to exploring each other's culture—be it through cooking traditional meals, watching films, or participating in cultural rituals. This allowed them to not just understand and appreciate their respective cultures but also to create new, hybrid traditions that were uniquely their own. Their relationship began to thrive, turning a potential stumbling block into a cornerstone of their partnership.

## Story 3: Jake and Liam - "Mindfulness Walks"

Jake and Liam had a fiery relationship. Both were passionate and quick-tempered, which led to frequent arguments. They came to therapy looking for ways to manage their anger and improve their communication skills.

One of the strategies proposed was to go on weekly "Mindfulness Walks" together. During these walks, they would focus on the experience of walking and nature, allowing space for quiet reflection. These walks became a sort of sanctuary for them. When conflicts arose later, they found it easier to tap into the calm they cultivated during these walks. Over time, they reported that their conflicts were less intense and easier to resolve, attributing this change largely to their newfound ritual.

## Story 4: Sarah and Mark - The Coffee Ritual

Sarah and Mark had been married for five years. They loved each other deeply but felt that the daily grind was pulling them apart. Seeking to reconnect, they came in for counseling. After discussing various aspects of their lives, they were recommended to find a simple but consistent ritual to strengthen their bond.

They chose a daily "coffee ritual." Every morning, before the hustle and bustle of the day, they would sit together for 20 minutes to enjoy a cup of coffee. No phones, no distractions—just the two of them and their coffee. It started as an experiment, but it quickly turned into a cherished daily experience that both eagerly anticipated. This simple act didn't just allow them to start their day together; it became a sacred time where they could share, plan, or simply be present with each other. The emotional impact of this small, daily ritual was profound.

These client stories illustrate how creating shared threads through rituals and shared experiences can significantly impact the quality and resilience of a relationship. Whether it's through daily practices, weekly events, or even less frequent but deeply meaningful shared experiences, couples can weave a stronger emotional and relational fabric that not only supports them during challenging times but also enriches their lives in moments of joy.

## Recommended Exercises

### Exercise 1: Ritual Creation Workshop

**Objective:**

To design your own ritual that you can incorporate into your daily or weekly life.

**Instructions:**

- **Brainstorming:** Both partners take 10 minutes to write down activities or experiences you both enjoy or would like to try. Keep these simple and achievable.
- **Discussion:** Share your lists with each other and see where your interests overlap or complement each other.

- **Design Your Ritual:** Using your shared interests, create a ritual that incorporates elements from both lists. Make sure it is something you can realistically commit to regularly.
- **Set Time and Frequency:** Decide when and how often you will practice this ritual. Mark it in your calendars to make it official.
- **Reflect:** After a month of following your newly created ritual, take time to discuss how it's affecting your relationship. Make any adjustments as necessary.

### Exercise 2: Shared Experience Journal

**Objective:**

To build a collection of shared experiences and memories.

**Instructions:**

- **Get a Journal:** Purchase or use an existing notebook to serve as your Shared Experience Journal.
- **Initial Entry:** Individually write down a memorable shared experience you cherish. Describe why it was meaningful to you.
- **Exchange and Reflect:** Share what you wrote with each other, and discuss your feelings and thoughts about those moments.

- **Keep Adding:** Whenever you have a shared experience that feels significant or particularly enjoyable, make a habit of jotting it down in the journal.
- **Monthly Reflection:** Sit down once a month to read through the journal together. Reflect on how these shared experiences are enriching your relationship.

**Exercise 3: Individuality Showcase**

**Objective:**

To celebrate each other's individual interests while building a shared experience.

**Instructions:**

- **List Your Interests:** Write down your individual interests that your partner is not familiar with.
- **Plan an Experience:** Take turns planning a date night or activity focused on introducing your partner to one of your interests.
- **Participate Wholeheartedly:** Even if the interest is not your cup of tea, engage with it sincerely, respecting your partner's passion for it.
- **Discuss:** After the experience, discuss what you learned about each other and how it felt to share in something uniquely important to one of you.

These exercises aim to create a blend of shared rituals and experiences while celebrating the individuality that makes each of you unique. The ultimate goal is to enrich your emotional connection and strengthen the bonds of your relationship.

## Life Story: A Tapestry of Rituals and Shared Experiences

If I were to look back on my life journey and the relationships that have shaped me, it would be impossible to ignore the role that rituals and shared experiences have played. Having traveled extensively, lived in multiple countries, and interacted with diverse cultures, the concept of shared experiences takes on an enriched meaning. Whether it's a traditional ritual in a remote village or a simple daily habit shared with a loved one, these practices create a sense of unity and emotional depth.

When I met my partner, we both had our own sets of routines and traditions formed through years of individual experiences. Merging these separate routines into a shared tapestry was not an overnight task; it required conscious effort, compromise, and a touch of creativity.

Take, for instance, our morning routine. I've always enjoyed the serenity of a quiet morning with a cup of coffee, meditating on the day ahead. My partner, on the other hand, found solace in listening to podcasts to greet the morning. We found a way to combine these rituals by dedicating our mornings to 'Quiet Time'—a meditative space where I could sip my coffee while enjoying the engaging discussions from the podcasts. It became our unique morning ritual, affirming our individual practices while creating a new, shared experience.

In professional settings as well, the power of shared experiences and rituals often comes to light. Individuals struggling with relationship issues frequently find it difficult to appreciate the small, everyday moments that make a relationship strong. They tend to overlook the power of shared rituals, like cooking together every Sunday or going for a monthly hike. These seemingly simple acts are often the glue that holds a relationship together when the grand gestures fall short.

During my travels, living in different cultures taught me the importance of shared experiences in building community bonds. The local traditions, whether it's a community dance, a shared meal, or even a communal work activity like farming, created a sense of belonging and mutual respect. These shared experiences transcend language and cultural barriers, highlighting a universal human craving for connection.

If there's anything my diverse life journey has taught me, it's that the strength of a relationship—be it between life partners, within a community, or among acquaintances—often lies in the seemingly small acts. It's in the shared laughter over an inside joke, the mutual excitement of exploring a new hiking trail, or the quiet understanding as you both enjoy a sunset. These are the threads that, when woven together, create a tapestry rich in emotional intimacy and resilience.

Through conscious effort, we can create these rituals and shared experiences to foster deeper emotional connections in our relationships, making them not just lasting but also enriching on multiple levels.

## Ending Note: Shared Threads

As we conclude this transformative chapter, let's take a moment to reflect on the myriad ways shared experiences and rituals can profoundly impact the quality of your relationship. Love, in its purest form, is an intricate tapestry woven from countless shared threads—each one a testament to the emotional investment, intellectual compatibility, and mutual respect between you and your partner. These threads can be grand or subtle, constant or evolving, but they are all vital in maintaining the tapestry's structural integrity and vibrant hues.

Your relationship is a living entity that requires ongoing nurturing. Like a garden, it can only flourish when tended to with care and intention. Shared rituals and experiences are the water and sunlight, the essential nutrients that help your emotional connection grow strong and bloom brightly. They are the antidotes to routine, the spice that prevents your interactions from becoming stagnant or predictable.

Incorporate what you have learned in this chapter into your life, and you'll find that these practices become more than just actions—they transform into meaningful rituals that nurture both your individual souls and your collective spirit. As you continue to thread these shared experiences into your everyday life, you'll find that you aren't just maintaining your relationship; you're elevating it, imbuing it with a depth and richness that allows both partners to flourish.

With being on the final chapter, we are at the end of this enlightening journey, but the work and the rewards are ongoing.

Here's to weaving a life filled with shared experiences, emotional intelligence, and enduring love, onward to the final chapter and beyond.

# Part V

# Conclusion

## Summary of Key Takeaways

As we arrive at the concluding chapter of this comprehensive exploration into the intricate dynamics of relationships, it's imperative to pause and reflect upon the myriad insights and lessons that have illuminated our path. This book has served as a roadmap, guiding us through the labyrinthine intricacies of love, intimacy, and the quest for individual identity within the context of a shared life.

Our odyssey commenced with a foundational understanding of the intricate dualities that love presents. We examined the psychological tug-of-war between our yearning for independence and an equally compelling need for intimacy. This initial exploration paved the way for a deeper understanding of how to strike a harmonious balance between these seemingly contradictory impulses.

From there, we delved into the enriching concept of self-awareness. As we highlighted, self-knowledge is far from a self-indulgent endeavor. Rather, it's a pivotal component that enhances the relational dynamic, allowing us to understand not just ourselves but also our partners in a more nuanced way. The exercise of crafting personal boundaries was presented as a natural extension of this self-awareness, a crucial practical step in safeguarding individual space even as we deepen our emotional connections.

Navigating further, we acknowledged the potential hazards of both excessive attachment and its opposite—extreme individuality. Far from simplistic cautionary tales, these chapters equipped us with a set of robust tools for building emotional resilience. They taught us to construct a reliable safety net capable of holding the weight of the relationship even when it is tested by the vicissitudes of life.

The subsequent part of our journey ushered us into the nuanced world of communication. Here, we moved beyond the mere mechanics of dialogue and ventured into the realm of emotional language. With the incorporation of strategies to express our needs, desires, and expectations transparently, we also embraced the art of empathic listening. The practice of tuning into our partner's emotional frequencies not only enriches our understanding but also deepens the level of intimacy in the relationship.

Our final destination in this exploration was the sanctified world of shared experiences and rituals. We discovered how the subtle weaving of shared memories, activities, and intentional gestures can become the connective tissue that binds a relationship together. We learned that these shared threads not only enrich the relationship but also serve to balance the scales between individuality and togetherness, allowing for a more nuanced, mature, and fulfilling partnership.

Throughout this narrative, a singular, profound truth has consistently resonated: a balanced relationship is not an erasure of individual complexities but a celebration of them. It isn't built on the quicksand of suppressed challenges; rather, it is fortified by the resilient ability to navigate those challenges with grace and skill. The relationship we aim to cultivate isn't characterized by an unhealthy fusion or by emotional detachment; it is a dynamic entity that lives and breathes in the shared yet respectful space between coming together and moving apart.

And so, with these multifaceted insights as our companions, we stand at the brink of endless relational possibilities, equipped with the wisdom to forge a partnership that is as enduring as it is enriching.

## Next Steps in Your Journey Toward Maintaining a Balanced Relationship

As we conclude this illuminative expedition through the complex landscape of relationships, it's crucial to recognize that the final pages of this book are not a termination but a commencement—a springboard propelling you toward an endless journey of relational refinement and growth. The pursuit of a balanced relationship is not a fixed goal but a perpetual, evolving endeavor, one that demands ongoing commitment, sustained effort, and, above all, an unwavering foundation of love. Below are some concrete, actionable steps to guide you as you continue on this transformative path:

- **Engage in Regular Check-Ins**: Don't let the insights you've gained become mere memories. Regularly revisit the concepts, strategies, and exercises elaborated in this book. Adapt and apply them to your evolving relational circumstances, like a gardener tending to an ever-changing garden, aware that each season brings new challenges and opportunities for growth.
- **Commit to Being a Lifelong Learner**: The 'Additional Resources' section at the end of this book is your navigational compass for sustained relational development. Treat it as a well of wisdom from which you can continually draw. Immerse yourself in further reading, partake in workshops, and enroll in relationship-enhancing courses to refine and expand your toolbox of relational skills.
- **Seek Professional Guidance When Necessary**: No journey is without its stumbling blocks or impassable terrains. When the relational path becomes too rocky or labyrinthine, remember that seeking professional guidance is not a sign of failure but an act of resourcefulness and commitment. External perspectives can often illuminate hidden aspects of your relationship and provide tailored strategies for moving forward.

- **Celebrate and Adapt to Change**: Both you and your partner are dynamic beings, constantly evolving in myriad ways. See this not as a challenge but as an opportunity. Celebrate each other's growth and consciously adapt your relationship to new phases of life, new interests, and emerging perspectives.
- **Promote Open Dialogue**: Take the time to share your insights and new understandings with your partner. Open, bilateral communication is the lifeblood of any thriving relationship. The more you both comprehend and implement these ideas, the more textured, resonant, and fulfilling your emotional life will become.
- **Nurture Emotional Resilience**: Equip yourself with coping mechanisms for the emotional ebbs and flows that inevitably characterize long-term relationships. Resilience is not just your shield but also your catalyst, propelling you through challenges toward greater intimacy and understanding.
- **Keep the Spark Alive**: Amid the day-to-day routines and responsibilities, never forget to nurture the romantic and emotional aspects of your relationship. Plan surprise dates, express your affection in creative ways, and keep rediscovering each other as if your relationship were a never-ending story.

With these multifaceted steps as your guide, you are not just well-equipped but profoundly empowered to continue this most sacred of journeys. You're setting forth on a path toward a relationship that transcends mere survival, one that thrives on emotional richness, depth, and beautiful complexity.

In closing, thank you for allowing me the honor of being a part of your transformative journey toward relational enlightenment and fulfillment. May your love story be an enduring tapestry of not just fleeting moments of happiness but of sustained, deeply rooted joy, mutual respect, and harmonious balance.

Wishing you a lifetime filled with boundless love, enriching experiences, and the epitome of balanced togetherness.

In the pages that follow, you'll find a curated list of recommended readings, workshops, and courses that align with the themes and lessons of this book. These resources further deepen your understanding and provide practical tools for relationship building.

# Additional Resources

**Chapter 1: The Dual Nature of Love: Autonomy and Intimacy**

**Books:**

- **"Hold Me Tight: Seven Conversations for a Lifetime of Love" by Dr. Sue Johnson**
- A deep dive into emotional bonds and how they affect relationship dynamics.
- **"The Road Less Traveled: A New Psychology of Love, Traditional Values and Spiritual Growth" by M. Scott Peck**
- Explores the complexities of love, including the balance between independence and intimacy.
- **"Attached: The New Science of Adult Attachment and How It Can Help You Find—and Keep—Love" by Amir Levine and Rachel Heller**
- Provides insights into different attachment styles and how they impact our need for closeness and autonomy.
- **"The Dance of Connection: How to Talk to Someone When You're Mad, Hurt, Scared, Frustrated, Insulted, Betrayed, or Desperate" by Harriet Lerner**

- Focuses on communication as a way to navigate the balance between autonomy and intimacy.

**Articles:**

- **"Self-Determination and the Paradox of Persistent Engagement"**
- A research article on how autonomy and competence are vital for sustaining engagement in activities, including relationships.
- **"Autonomy in Romantic Relationships: A Review"**
- Discusses the importance of maintaining autonomy in a relationship and its positive outcomes.
- **"The Importance of Maintaining Emotional Intimacy"**
- An article discussing why emotional intimacy is crucial for the longevity of romantic relationships.

**Online Courses:**

- **"Love and Connection: The Science of Successful Relationships"**
- A course that combines scientific insights and practical exercises to deepen intimacy and maintain individuality in relationships.
- **"Building Emotional Intelligence: How to Build and Maintain Emotional Balance in a Hyper-Connected World"**

- A course that discusses the importance of self-awareness, emotional regulation, and how to keep a balanced relationship.

**Podcasts:**

- **"The Art of Charm: Relationship Theory"**
- Offers insights on maintaining a healthy balance between being an individual and being in a partnership.
- **"Where Should We Begin? with Esther Perel"**
- Psychotherapist Esther Perel discusses real-life relationship problems, including the challenge of balancing intimacy with autonomy.

**Websites and Apps:**

- **Gottman Relationship Checkup**
- A thorough relationship assessment tool that can highlight areas where you might need more autonomy or intimacy.
- **Relish**
- A relationship coaching app that offers personalized lessons to improve your relationship, including balancing autonomy and intimacy.

**Chapter 2: The Mirror and the Window**

**Books:**

- "Self-Awareness (H.B.R. Emotional Intelligence Series)" by Harvard Business Review
- "Emotional Intelligence 2.0" by Travis Bradberry and Jean Greaves
- "The Untethered Soul" by Michael A. Singer
- "Daring Greatly: How the Courage to Be Vulnerable Transforms the Way We Live, Love, Parent, and Lead" by Brené Brown

**Online Courses:**

- "Becoming Self-Aware" on Coursera
- "Building Emotional Intelligence" on Udemy
- "Interpersonal Communication Skills" on LinkedIn Learning

Articles and Blogs:

- "The Importance of Self-Awareness, and How to Become More Self-Aware" - Psychology Today
- "Understanding Emotional Triggers: A New Approach to Self-Control" - Scientific American
- "What Self-Awareness Really Is (and How to Cultivate It)" - Harvard Business Review

**Podcasts:**

- "Unlocking Us" by Brené Brown

- "The Tony Robbins Podcast: Emotional Triggers and How to Control Them"
- "The Art of Charm: Boosting Self-Awareness"

**Apps for Mindfulness and Self-Awareness:**

- Headspace - Mindfulness and meditation exercises
- Insight Timer - Meditation, Sleep, and Self-Awareness
- MyLife Meditation - Focus on emotional check-ins

**Videos and Documentaries:**

- "The Power of Vulnerability" - T.E.D. Talk by Brené Brown
- "How to become more self-aware" - TEDx Talk by Tasha Eurich
- "What is Emotional Intelligence?" - YouTube video by Psychology Today

By exploring these resources, you can deepen your understanding of self-awareness and how it influences your relationship. Whether you prefer books, articles, or interactive courses, there's a wealth of knowledge available to help you on your journey.

## Chapter 3: Personal Spaces: Crafting and Sustaining Boundaries

**Books**

- "Boundaries in Marriage" by Dr. Henry Cloud and Dr. John Townsend
- This book delves deep into the concept of boundaries, specifically within the context of marital relationships.
- "Boundaries: Where You End and I Begin" by Anne Katherine
- A comprehensive guide to understanding the importance of boundaries and how to establish them.
- "The Assertiveness Workbook: How to Express Your Ideas and Stand Up for Yourself at Work and in Relationships" by Randy J. Paterson
- This workbook provides practical exercises to improve your assertiveness, which is crucial in setting and maintaining boundaries.

**Articles**

- "The Importance of Personal Boundaries" - Psychology Today
- An article that succinctly discusses the essential nature of boundaries in interpersonal relationships.
- "How to Create Healthy Boundaries" - Harvard Health Blog
- A scientific perspective on the importance of boundaries and how to establish them.

**Websites and Online Courses**

- "Setting Boundaries in Relationships: A Course" - Udemy
- This online course covers the nitty-gritty of setting boundaries and maintaining them.
- BetterHelp
- Online counseling services that offer one-on-one consultations to help you understand and establish your boundaries.

**Podcasts**

- "Where Should We Begin? with Esther Perel"
- Renowned relationship therapist Esther Perel explores real-life relationship dynamics, often touching upon the subject of boundaries.
- "The Boundaries.Me Podcast" by Dr. Henry Cloud
- Each episode offers a deep dive into different types of boundaries and how to make them work in various aspects of your life.

Feel free to explore these resources at your own pace, and remember: Your journey toward understanding and implementing boundaries is your own, so take the steps that feel right for you and your relationship.

**Chapter 4: The Quicksand of Over-Attachment: When Togetherness Turns Toxic**

To delve deeper into the themes discussed in this chapter, the following resources can offer further insight, guidance, and practical tips on navigating the complex terrain of over-attachment in relationships.

**Books:**

- "Attached: The New Science of Adult Attachment and How It Can Help You Find – and Keep – Love" by Amir Levine and Rachel Heller
- "Boundaries in Marriage" by Dr. Henry Cloud and Dr. John Townsend
- "Codependent No More" by Melody Beattie
- "Hold Me Tight: Seven Conversations for a Lifetime of Love" by Dr. Sue Johnson

**Articles:**

- "How to Maintain Individuality While Building a Strong Relationship" - Psychology Today
- "5 Signs You're Too Attached To Your Partner" - HuffPost
- "The Importance of Personal Space in a Relationship" - Medium

**Podcasts:**

- "The Art of Charm: How to Read Minds" - Episode 748
- "The Gottman Institute: The Science of Love"
- "The Minimalists: Letting Go of Attachment"

**Webinars and Online Courses:**

- "Building Healthy Relationships: From "Me" to "We""
- "Personal Boundaries: Life Skills for Emotional Safety"
- "Emotional Intelligence: Managing Over-Attachment"

**Apps:**

- "Headspace" - For mindfulness techniques that can help improve self-awareness.
- "Lasting" - A marriage health app designed to help couples build healthier and happier relationships.

These resources cover a variety of formats to suit your preferred style of learning. Whether you are a reader, a listener, or an interactive learner, these tools will help you better understand the concepts of attachment, boundaries, and maintaining a healthy balance in your relationship.

**Chapter 5: Isolation Chambers: The Pitfalls of Excessive Individuality**

**Books:**

- **"Hold Me Tight" by Dr. Sue Johnson**
- An excellent read on emotional bonds and attachment in relationships.
- **"The Seven Principles for Making Marriage Work" by Dr. John Gottman**
- This book provides scientific insights into a relationship's dynamics and offers practical advice for maintaining balance.
- **"Codependent No More" by Melody Beattie**
- If you find that your sense of self is being overshadowed in a relationship, this book is a must-read.

**Websites and Online Courses:**

- **Relate.org.uk**
- Offers a variety of articles and online courses about relationship health, including the importance of individuality.
- **The Gottman Institute Blog**
- A treasure trove of articles by experts on maintaining the balance between "me" and "we" in relationships.
- **Coursera: Maintaining a Balanced Relationship**
- An online course that delves into the intricacies of keeping a relationship balanced.

**Podcasts:**

- **"The Art of Charm"**
- Episodes often explore the topic of maintaining your individuality in relationships.
- **"Relationship Alive!"**
- A podcast that covers many aspects of relationships, including the dangers of excessive individuality.

**YouTube Channels:**

- **School of Life**
- Offers a philosophical take on relationships and the balance between individuality and unity.

- **TEDx Talks**
- Features a variety of talks on relationships, including the importance of maintaining your own space.

**Apps:**

- **CouplesCounseling**

  Offers exercises to help maintain balance in a relationship.
- **Reflectly**

  A personal journal that can help you monitor your thoughts and feelings, assisting in maintaining a balanced relationship.

By exploring these resources, you can gain deeper insights into the complexities of balancing individuality and unity in relationships. Use them as tools to help maintain a healthy equilibrium, both for yourself and your partnership.

## Chapter 6: Emotional Resilience: Your Relationship's Safety Net

**Books:**

- "Emotional Agility" by Susan David
- "Daring Greatly" by Brené Brown
- "The Relationship Cure" by John Gottman
- "The Road Less Traveled" by M. Scott Peck
- "Radical Acceptance" by Tara Brach

**Online Courses:**

- "The Science of Well-Being" offered by Yale University on Coursera
- "Mindfulness and Resilience to Stress at Work" offered by Berkeley on edX
- "Building Emotional Intelligence" on LinkedIn Learning

**Podcasts:**

- "The Art of Charm"
- "The Tony Robbins Podcast"
- "Unlocking Us" by Brené Brown

- "The Science of Happiness" by the Greater Good Science Center

**Apps:**

- Headspace – For Mindfulness and Meditation
- Couple - Relationship App for Two
- Moodpath - Emotional and Mental Health
- Smiling Mind - Stress, Anxiety and Well-being

**Websites:**

- Mindful.org – Offers a range of articles and exercises on mindfulness and emotional intelligence
- Gottman Institute Blog – Offers relationship advice grounded in decades of research.
- American Psychological Association's Resilience Page – Provides research and tips on building resilience.

Support Groups and Therapists:

- Local couple's therapy or counseling services can provide tailored, in-person support.
- Online forums and social media groups dedicated to relationship improvement and emotional health can offer community support.

These resources are designed to complement the content of this chapter, providing you with additional tools and perspectives to deepen your understanding of emotional resilience in relationships.

## Chapter 7: Decoding the Language of Love: Expressing Needs and Desires

### Books

- "Nonviolent Communication: A Language of Life" by Marshall B. Rosenberg - A seminal book that lays out the principles of compassionate communication.
- "Men Are from Mars, Women Are from Venus" by John Gray - Although somewhat dated, this book explores gender differences in communication.
- "Hold Me Tight: Seven Conversations for a Lifetime of Love" by Dr. Sue Johnson - Offers practical conversations for couples to improve their emotional connection.

### Articles

- "The 5 Love Languages Explained" by Gary Chapman - A quick read that covers the principles behind different love languages.
- "How to Improve Your Communication Skills" - A comprehensive article that provides actionable tips for better communication.

### Podcasts

- "The Art of Charm" - Various episodes focus on improving social dynamics and communication skills.
- "Relationship Alive!" - This podcast often covers the nuances of effective communication in relationships.

**Online Courses**

- "Improving Communication Skills" by Coursera - A structured course that dives deep into the mechanics of effective communication.
- "The Relationship Communication Course" by Udemy - Specifically designed for couples, this course aims to eliminate misunderstandings and enhance verbal exchanges.

**Apps**

- "Relish" - A relationship coaching and self-care app that includes modules on improving communication.
- "Lasting" - An app designed for couples therapy that includes sessions on communication skills.

**YouTube Channels**

- "The School of Life" - Offers multiple videos tackling various aspects of relationships, including communication.

- "T.E.D. Talks" - Search for talks on "Relationship Communication" for a selection of expert presentations on the subject.

**Websites**

- Gottman Institute Blog - A wealth of articles and resources specifically focused on couple's therapy and communication.
- Psychology Today's Section on Communication - Provides articles from different experts on improving dialogue in relationships.

Feel free to dive into these resources to enrich your understanding and application of effective communication strategies in relationships.

**Chapter 8: The Echo Chamber: Developing Active Listening and Empathy Skills**

**Books**

- **"Nonviolent Communication: A Language of Life" by Marshall B. Rosenberg**
- A foundational book for anyone interested in understanding the core principles of empathetic communication.

- **"Crucial Conversations: Tools for Talking When Stakes Are High" by Kerry Patterson, Joseph Grenny, Ron McMillan, and Al Switzler**
- This book offers a step-by-step approach for effectively communicating in high-stakes or emotionally charged situations.
- **"You're Not Listening: What You're Missing and Why It Matters" by Kate Murphy**
- This book dives deep into the intricacies of listening as an art form, highlighting what we stand to gain from truly engaging with those around us.

**Online Courses**

- **Coursera: "Improving Communication Skills" by University of Pennsylvania**
- A comprehensive course that covers both active listening and effective communication techniques.

- **Udemy: "Practical Empathy Training"**
- A focused course that teaches the basics of emotional and cognitive empathy.

**Workshops**

- **Gottman Institute Workshops**
- Specializes in relationships and offers workshops in active listening and empathetic communication.

- **Center for Nonviolent Communication**
- Offers workshops and seminars specifically focused on nonviolent communication techniques.

**Podcasts**

- **"The Art of Charm"**
- Covers various aspects of effective communication, including active listening and empathy.
- **"On Being"**
- Explores the human side of things, often touching on themes of empathy, understanding, and meaningful conversation.

**Websites & Blogs**

- **Psychology Today's Communication Section**
- A valuable resource for articles on active listening, empathy, and effective communication.
- Mindful.org
- Offers insights into mindful listening and how to practice empathy in daily life.

**YouTube Channels**

- **TEDx Talks on Active Listening and Empathy**
- Multiple TEDx speakers discuss the importance of these skills and how to develop them.
- **The School of Life**

- Offers several videos on how to improve your emotional intelligence, including communication skills and empathy.

By tapping into these resources, you'll further enrich your understanding and mastery of the principles laid out in this chapter. Whether you're reading, watching, or actively participating, each resource can offer you additional layers of insight into the transformative power of active listening and empathy.

**Chapter 9: Shared Threads: Rituals and Experiences that Enrich Your Relationship**

**Books**

- **"The Five Love Languages" by Gary Chapman** - Understand how different expressions of love can act as shared experiences to strengthen your relationship.
- **"Hold Me Tight: Seven Conversations for a Lifetime of Love" by Dr. Sue Johnson** - Explores emotional connectivity and how daily rituals can sustain it.
- **"The Rituals: Simple Practices to Cultivate Well-Being, Deepen Relationships, and Discover Your True Purpose" by Natalie MacNeil** - A guide to creating your own personal and relationship rituals.

**Websites and Apps**

- **Gottman Institute Blog** - Contains articles and exercises on maintaining relationship health, including the importance of rituals.
- Gottman Institute Blog
- **Couple** - An app for couples to share messages, experiences, and reminders to engage in relationship-strengthening activities.
- Couple App
- **Lasting** - Offers personalized relationship training exercises, including activities couples can do together.
- Lasting

**Online Courses**

- **"Building a Strong Relationship and Marriage" on Coursera** - Covers the fundamentals of maintaining a lasting relationship, including the importance of shared activities.
- **"The Art of Connection" on Udemy** - Focuses on communication and shared experiences to create a strong bond.
- **"Positive Psychology" on Coursera** - Teaches the scientific aspects of happiness and well-being, including the importance of shared positive experiences.

**Workshops and Retreats**

- **The Couples Institute** - Offers various workshops that often include the crafting of shared experiences and rituals.
- The Couples Institute
- **Imago Relationship Workshops** - Aimed at deepening emotional connections through shared experiences.
- Imago Workshops

**Podcasts**

- **"The Relationship School Podcast"** - Features episodes discussing the importance of rituals and shared activities in relationships.
- **"Where Should We Begin? with Esther Perel"** - Provides real-life relationship stories, some of which focus on the creation and maintenance of shared rituals.

**Documentaries**

- **"Happy" (2011)** - Explores what makes people happy, including the importance of relationships and shared experiences.

**YouTube Channels**

- **"Jay Shetty on Relationships"** - Provides tips and exercises for couples looking to enhance their relationship through shared experiences.

By engaging with these resources, you can further enrich your understanding of how shared experiences and personal rituals contribute to a healthy, loving relationship.

www.ingramcontent.com/pod-product-compliance
Lightning Source LLC
LaVergne TN
LVHW041201150826
845673LV00001B/251

* 9 7 8 1 9 1 7 0 5 4 2 1 8 *